Landmark Productions and **The Everyman**
in association with
the **Abbey Theatre** and **Cork Midsummer Festival**
present

T0352635

BY **LOUISE O'NEILL**

ADAPTED BY **MEADHBH McHUGH**
IN COLLABORATION WITH **ANNABELLE COMYN**

The world premiere of *Asking for It* took place at
The Everyman, Cork, on 15 June 2018.

Co-commissioned by The Abbey Theatre.
Funded through an Arts Council Open Call Award.

 **LANDMARK**

Landmark Productions is one of Ireland's leading theatre producers. Led by Anne Clarke, the company produces wide-ranging and ambitious work in Ireland and tours Irish work abroad.

Since its first production in 2004, the company has produced thirty-one plays, including seventeen world premieres and seven Irish premieres.

Its productions include the Irish premieres of David Hare's *Skylight*, Edward Albee's *The Goat, or Who is Sylvia?*, David Harrower's *Knives in Hens* and his Olivier Award-winning play *Blackbird*.

The company's recent work includes the world premieres of Mark O'Rowe's *The Approach* and Paul Howard's *Postcards from the Ledge*, together with several productions by Enda Walsh: *The Walworth Farce*, starring Brendan Gleeson, Brian Gleeson and Domhnall Gleeson; the world premieres of *The Last Hotel* and *The Second Violinist*, two operas by Donnacha Dennehy and Enda Walsh, both co-produced with Irish National Opera; and the multi award-winning musical *Once*, which played at the Olympia Theatre for three successive summers.

Landmark's award-winning co-productions with Galway International Arts Festival include the world premieres of Conall Morrison's *Woyzeck in Winter*, which subsequently toured to the Barbican in London, together with Enda Walsh's *Arlington, Ballyturk* and *Misterman*. All three plays subsequently toured to St Ann's Warehouse in New York, and *Misterman* and *Ballyturk* were seen at the National Theatre in London.

Grief is the Thing with Feathers by Max Porter, adapted and directed by Enda Walsh and starring Cillian Murphy, produced by Complicité and Wayward Productions in association with Landmark Productions and Galway International Arts Festival, had its world premiere in Galway in March 2018.

Landmark received the Judges' Special Award in The Irish Times Irish Theatre Awards for 2011, in recognition of its 'sustained excellence in programming and for developing imaginative partnerships to bring quality theatre to the Irish and international stage'. Anne Clarke received the Special Tribute Award in 2015, in recognition of her work as 'a producer of world-class theatre in the independent sector in Ireland'.

Landmark is supported by the Arts Council and Dublin City Council. Its international touring is supported by Culture Ireland.

Producer | Anne Clarke
Associate Producer | Sara Cregan

www.landmarkproductions.ie

THE EVERYMAN

The Everyman is a non-profit company that produces and presents the best in Irish and international performance for Cork and Irish audiences. Our beautiful theatre is a 650-seat listed building and a jewel of late Victorian architecture, which celebrated its 120th birthday in 2017.

Recent theatre productions and co-productions include the world premieres of *The Nightingale and the Rose* (2018) – a new opera by John O'Brien after Oscar Wilde; *Asking for It* by Louise O'Neill (2018); Kevin Barry's *Autumn Royal* (2017 and national tour 2018); the Irish premiere of Lynda Radley's *Futureproof* (2017); as well as critically acclaimed revivals of Martin McDonagh's *The Lonesome West* (2018), Brian Friel's *Dancing at Lughnasa* (2017), Frank McGuinness' *The Factory Girls* (2016), Sean O'Casey's *Juno and the Paycock* (2016), Charles Gounod's *Faust* (2015), David Greig's *The Strange Undoing of Prudencia Hart* (2015) and Brian Friel's *Lovers* (2015).

The Everyman is proud to be supported by the Arts Council and Cork City Council.

Executive Director | Sean Kelly
Artistic Director | Julie Kelleher

www.everymancork.com

ABBEY THEATRE
AMHARCLANN NA MAINISTREACH

Inspired by the revolutionary ideals of its founders and its rich canon of Irish dramatic writing, the Abbey Theatre's Mission is to imaginatively engage with all of Irish society through the production of ambitious, courageous and new theatre in all its forms. The Abbey Theatre commits to lead in the telling of the whole Irish story, in English and in Irish, and affirms that it is a theatre for the entire island of Ireland and for all its people. In every endeavour, the Abbey Theatre promotes inclusiveness, diversity and equality.

CORK MIDSUMMER FESTIVAL

Cork Midsummer Festival is an annual multi-disciplinary arts festival that uses the city of Cork as its backdrop and inspiration, featuring performances and events for audiences of all ages. Its programme provides diverse opportunities for participation and engagement, supports the development of emerging artists across all artforms, and provides a unique platform for local and national artists, while also bringing acclaimed international work to Cork for local audiences to experience.

BY **LOUISE O'NEILL**

ADAPTED BY **MEADHBH McHUGH**
IN COLLABORATION WITH **ANNABELLE COMYN**

CAST (in order of appearance)

EMMA	**Lauren Coe**
MAM	**Ali White**
ZOE	**Venetia Bowe**
CONOR	**Frank Blake**
ALI	**Síle Maguire**
MAGGIE	**Amy McElhatton**
SEAN	**Seán Doyle**
ELI	**Kwaku Fortune**
DYLAN	**Darragh Shannon**
PAUL	**Charlie Maher**
DAD	**Frank McCusker**
BRYAN	**Paul Mescal**
VOICES	**Shane Casey**
	Julie Kelleher
	Jonathan White

The play is set in Ballinatoom, West Cork.
There will be one interval of 15 minutes.

Director	**Annabelle Comyn**
Set Designer	**Paul O'Mahony**
Costume Designer	**Niamh Lunny**
Lighting Designer	**Sinead McKenna**
Sound Designer	**Philip Stewart**
Video Designer	**Jack Phelan**
Movement Director	**Sue Mythen**
Hair and Make-Up	**Val Sherlock**
Voice Coach	**Cathal Quinn**
Assistant Director	**Jack Reardon**
Production Manager	**Eamonn Fox**
Deputy Production Manager	**Tom Rohan**
Stage Manager	**Clare Howe**
Assistant Stage Manager	**Emma Coen**
Costume Supervisor	**Sinead Lawlor**
Wardrobe Maintenance	**Ciara Geaney**
Set Construction	**TPS**
Producers	**Anne Clarke** | Landmark
	Julie Kelleher | The Everyman
Associate Producer	**Sara Cregan**
Publicists	**Sinead O'Doherty**
	Kearney Melia Barker
Marketing	**Sinead McPhillips**
Photographers	**Hugh O'Conor** | photoshoot
	Patrick Redmond | production
Graphic Design	**Gareth Jones**

www.askingforit.ie

Louise O' Neill

Louise O'Neill grew up in Clonakilty, a small town in West Cork. Her first novel, *Only Ever Yours*, was released in 2014. *Only Ever Yours* went on to win the Sunday Independent Newcomer of the Year at the 2014 Bord Gáis Energy Irish Book Awards; the Children's Books Ireland Eilís Dillon Award for a First Children's Book; and The Bookseller's inaugural YA Book Prize 2015.

Louise's second novel, *Asking for It*, was published in September 2015 to widespread critical acclaim. She went on to win the Specsavers' Senior Children's Book of the Year at the 2015 Irish Book Awards, the Literature Prize at Irish Tatler's Women of the Year Awards, and the American Library Association's Michael L. Printz Award. *Asking for It* was voted Book of the Year at the Irish Book Awards 2015 and spent 52 weeks in the Irish top 10 bestseller list. The New York Times called it 'riveting and essential' and The Guardian named O'Neill 'the best YA fiction writer alive today'. Both novels have been optioned for screen.

O'Neill's first novel for adults, *Almost Love*, was published in March 2018. *The Surface Breaks*, her feminist re-imagining of *The Little Mermaid*, was released in May 2018, and has been shortlisted for an Irish Book Award and for the Specsavers National Book Awards in the UK.

Meadhbh McHugh

Meadhbh McHugh is an Irish playwright and writer living in New York. Meadhbh's debut play, *Helen and I*, was staged by Druid Theatre Company in 2016 at the Mick Lally Theatre in Galway. The play was also performed as part of the Dublin Theatre Festival and was nominated for the Stewart Parker Trust Award in 2016. Meadhbh's debut radio play, *April Showers*, won a PJ O'Connor Award for new writing and was broadcast on RTÉ Radio One in 2014. She holds a B.A. in Drama Studies and English Literature from Trinity College Dublin; an M.F.A in Playwriting from The Lir Academy, Dublin; and an M.Phil. in Theatre from Columbia University in New York, where she currently teaches writing.

Annabelle Comyn | Director

Annabelle Comyn is an award-winning Irish theatre director, Artistic Director of Hatch Theatre Company, and Director in Residence at The Lir, the National Academy of Dramatic Arts, Ireland.

She has been directing for theatre for 24 years, and has worked with The Abbey, Druid, The Gate, Dublin Theatre Festival and the Lyric Theatre, Belfast among others.

Productions include *Dubliners: an opera* (OTC); *Crestfall* by Mark O'Rowe (Druid, as part of the 2017 Galway International Arts Festival); *Helen and I* (Druid); *The Wake, Hedda Gabler, Major Barbara, The House* (Irish Times Irish Theatre Award for Best Director), *Pygmalion, A Number* and *Blue/Orange* (Abbey Theatre); *Dancing at Lughnasa* (Lyric Theatre, Belfast and DTF); *Contractions* and *The Sit* (Bewley's Café Theatre); and *Look Back in Anger* and *The Vortex* (Gate Theatre, Dublin).

For Hatch Theatre Company, plays include *The Talk of the Town* (in a co-production with Landmark Productions and Dublin Theatre Festival), *Love and Money, Further Than the Furthest Thing, Cruel and Tender, Pyrenees, Blood* and *The Country*.

Paul O'Mahony | Set Designer

Previous designs for Landmark include *Breaking Dad, Underneath the Lintel* and *The Talk of the Town* (a co-production with Hatch Theatre Company and Dublin Theatre Festival). Designs for The Everyman include *Futureproof* during Cork Midsummer Festival.

Other theatre designs include *Look Back in Anger, Wuthering Heights, The Vortex, An Enemy of the People, Little Women, Faith Healer* (Gate Theatre); *The Wake, Town is Dead, Hedda Gabler, Major Barbara, The House, Pygmalion, Macbeth, The Seafarer, Fool for Love, Saved, Blue/Orange* (Abbey Theatre); *Nora, The Seagull* (Corn Exchange); *Love and Money, Further Than the Furthest Thing, Pyrenees, Blood, The Country* (Hatch); *The Importance of Being Earnest, Solemn Mass for a Full Moon in Summer, Is this About Sex?, Don Carlos* (Rough Magic); *This is Our Youth, Wedding Day at the Cro-Magnons, Roberto Zucco, This is Not a Life, Pale Angel, Self-Accusation* (Bedrock Productions); and *Medea* (Siren Productions). Operas include *Dubliners* and *Acis and Galatea* (Opera Theatre Company); and *Rusalka* (Lyric Opera).

He has also designed for the Lyric Theatre Belfast, Everyman Liverpool, The Ark/ Theatre Lovett, Calipo, Peer to Peer, Prime Cut Productions, b*spoke, Upstate, Cork Opera House, CoisCéim Dance Theatre and The Lir.

Paul trained at Motley Theatre Design Course, London.

Niamh Lunny | Costume Designer

Niamh is the recipient of the 2018-19 Arts Council / Jerome Hynes Scholarship on the Clore Leadership Programme. Prior to this she was Head of Costume at the Abbey Theatre for eleven years, during which time she designed extensively for the Abbey and Peacock Theatres as well as serving four years on the Board of Directors.

She has designed for ANU, Fishamble Theatre Company, The Performance Corporation, NAYD, Rough Magic and The Ark, among many other theatre, film, television and production companies. She has also worked collaboratively and independently on a diverse range of commissions from events to merchandise. She spent four years as the Costume Co-ordinator at the Samuel Beckett Theatre.

Niamh is a graduate of Limerick College of Art and Design.

Sinead McKenna | Lighting Designer

Sinead has received two Irish Times Irish Theatre Awards for Best Lighting Design and a Drama Desk nomination for Best Lighting Design for a Musical.

Previous designs for Landmark include *The Approach, Howie the Rookie, Greener, October, The Last Days of the Celtic Tiger* and *Blackbird*.

Recent designs include *Grace Jones - Bloodlight and Bami* (Blinder Films); *Angela's Ashes* (Pat Moylan Productions); *Futureproof* (Everyman, Cork); and *Nivelli's War* (Cahoots NI/ New Victory Theatre).

Other theatre designs include *Richard III* and *Uncle Vanya* (West Yorkshire Playhouse); *Beckett/Pinter/Friel Festival, Private Lives, Juno and the Paycock* and *The Gigli Concert* (Gate Theatre); *Maz and Bricks* (Fishamble); *Fire Below* (Lyric/Abbey Theatre); *The Wake, Othello, Aristocrats, Quietly, Finders Keepers* (Abbey Theatre); *Famished Castle, Travesties, Improbable Frequency* (Drama Desk nomination), *Life is a Dream* and *Attempts on her Life* (Rough Magic); *The Wolf and Peter, Agnes, Pageant* (CoisCéim); *Invitation to a Journey* (CoisCéim/Fishamble/Crash Ensemble); *La Traviata* (Malmö Opera House); and *The Rape of Lucretia* (IYO).

She has also worked with Corn Exchange, Druid, Opera Ireland, Opera Theatre Company, Decadent, Gare Saint Lazare, Corn Exchange, Thisispopbaby, Siren, Second Age, The Performance Corporation, Semper Fi and Gúna Nua.

Philip Stewart | Sound Designer

Philip has written music and sound design for a broad range of media including theatre, sculptural and sound installations, dance, shorts, and documentary film-making. He studied composition under Donnacha Dennehy and Roger Doyle.

Recent theatre credits include *Crestfall* by Mark O'Rowe (Druid); *The Wake* by Tom Murphy, *Conservatory* by Michael West, *Hedda Gabler* by Henrik Ibsen, *Quietly* by Owen McCafferty (Abbey Theatre); and *The Approach* by Mark O'Rowe, *Breaking Dad* by Paul Howard and *Howie the Rookie* by Mark O'Rowe (Landmark Productions).

He has been nominated for an Irish Times Irish Theatre Award for his work on *The Early Bird* by Leo Butler (Natural Shocks) and *An Enemy of the People* by Henrik Ibsen (Gate Theatre).

Jack Phelan | Video Designer

Jack is a video artist and technologist who specialises in integrating new visual ideas and technology into live performance. Recent productions include *Bluebeard's Castle* (Irish National Opera); *The Second Violinist* by Enda Walsh and Donnacha Dennehy (Landmark / INO); *Arlington* by Enda Walsh (Landmark / GIAF); and *Money* (Thisispopbaby). He worked with The Corn Exchange and actor Paul Reid on *Man of Valour* to create a neo-noir world of atmospherics and shadow using 3D modelling and lighting with projection. Also with The Corn Exchange, Jack combined wireless cameras and image processing to bring the audience closer to the cast of the award-winning *Freefall*. Other theatrical credits include *Alice in Funderland* (Thisispopbaby / Abbey Theatre); *Dubliners* (The Corn Exchange / Dublin Theatre Festival); *The Shawshank Redemption* (Lane Productions); *The Lulu House* and *Macbeth* (Siren Productions); *Love and Money* (Hatch Theatre) and *Woman and Scarecrow* (Siren / Abbey).

Jack was also a core member of the creative / tech team behind Playhouse, a large-scale interactive lighting installation for public expression. Produced for Dublin Theatre Festival in 2009, Playhouse turned Dublin's Liberty Hall into an 11 storey, full-colour video display that displayed animations submitted by the public to music synchronised with Dublin City FM.

Sue Mythen | Movement Director

Based in Dublin, Sue works as a movement director in theatre, opera and film. She is Head of Movement at The Lir Academy, TCD.

Recent credits include *The Lost O'Casey* (ANU / Abbey / DTF); *If We Got Some More Cocaine I Could Tell You How I Love You* (Project Arts Centre); *On Raftery's Hill* (Abbey); *Crestfall* (Druid); *Private Peaceful* (Verdant Productions); *Radamisto* (NI Opera); *The White Devil* (Shakespeare's Globe, London); and *The Heiress* (The Gate).

Other credits include *The Sin Eaters, On Corporation Street, Sunder, Pals: The Irish at Gallipoli* and *Angel Meadow* (ANU); *Oedipus, The Shadow of a Gunman* (Abbey / Lyric), *R.U.R* (YTI / Abbey), *Hedda Gabler, Twelfth Night, The Plough and the Stars, Heartbreak House, 16 Possible Glimpses, The House, The Rivals, Pygmalion* and *Major Barbara* (Abbey Theatre); *Displaced*, which she co-created with Natasha Martina, and winner of best original script at SATA awards, Canada, nominated for five awards at 2015 Montreal Fringe Festival and Singapore Festival 2018; *Elektra* (Canadian Opera Company), Toronto; *Worstward Ho* (Mouth on Fire / Theatre X_cai, Tokyo); *Semele* (RIAM); and *Dead Man Walking* (Opera Ireland).

Acknowledgements

Landmark Productions and The Everyman would like to thank Lorraine Maye and all at Cork Midsummer Festival; Neil Murray and Graham McLaren, together with Aoife Brady, Jen Coppinger, Lisa Farrelly, Chris Hay, Phil Kingston, Sarah Ling, Sarah Lynch, Paddy Jo Malpas and all at the Abbey Theatre; Saoirse Anton; Azzurri; Lara Beach; Sayonara Bittencourt; Lorraine Brennan; Tim Burke and all at Coláiste Choilm, Ballincollig; Siobhán Burke; Shane Casey; Hugh Chaloner; Liam Clancy; Niall Cleary, Ravnita Joyce and all at Fighting Words Cork at Graffiti Theatre; Rose Cobbe; Maria Collard; Frank Commins; Aidan Connolly, Rachael Gilkey and all at Irish Arts Center; Rachel Conway; Emma Creaner; Cue One; Mary Crilly at Cork Sexual Violence Centre; Richard Cook, Jasmine Daines Pilgrem, Morris Epstein and Jonathan Shankey at Lisa Richards; Martin Davoren at Sexual Health Centre Cork; Druid Theatre Company; Clare Dunne; Monica Ennis; Rowan Finken; Tim Gannon and Graham Seely at Gansee Films; Éanna Hardwicke; Irish School Badges; Niall Kelly; Sean Kelly, Naomi Daly and all at the Everyman; Eoin Kilkenny; Made for Stage; Laura MacNaughton and all at the O'Reilly Theatre; Aoife McCollum; Doreen Meehan; Miriam Molloy; Janet Moran; Josh Muldoon; Susannah Norris; Barry O'Brien; Hugh O'Conor; Alison Oliver; Conall Ó Riain; Gavin O'Sullivan and all at Irish National Opera; Trevor Price; Nick Quinn; Colm Robinson; Bella Rodrigues; Gilly Sanguinetti; Shirley Scott; Nuria Segura; Chris Somers; Stage Sound Services; Oddie Sherwin; Kate Staddon; Rachel West; Eleanor White; and Jonathan White.

Asking for It was funded by The Arts Council / An Chomhairle Ealaíon through an Open Call Award.

Cast

Frank Blake | CONOR

Originally from Co. Clare, Frank is a graduate of The Lir.

Recent theatre credits include *Richard III* (Druid) and *Dublin by Lamplight* (Corn Exchange).

Recent film and TV credits include *Game of Thrones* (HBO); *The Frankenstein Chronicles* (ITV / A&E Networks) and *Rebellion* (RTÉ).

Venetia Bowe | ZOE

Venetia has most recently been cast as the lead in Oonagh Kearney's experimental dance short, *Five Letters to the Stranger who will Dissect my Brain*, a collaboration with Junk Ensemble based on a poem by Doireann Ní Ghríofa.

Theatre credits include the national tour of Brokentalkers' acclaimed *This Beach* and the role of Emmy in *Nora*, a version of Ibsen's *A Doll's House* adapted by Belinda McKeon and Annie Ryan for The Corn Exchange.

Venetia holds a Bachelor in Acting from The Lir Academy at Trinity College Dublin (in partnership with RADA).

Lauren Coe | EMMA

Lauren is a graduate of The Lir.

Recent theatre credits include *A Room with a View* (Theatre Royal Bath); *A View from the Bridge* and *Romeo and Juliet* (Gate Theatre); and *Punk Rock* (Lyric Theatre, Belfast).

TV credits include *Call the Midwife*; *Troy – Fall of the City*; *The Halcyon*; *Camelot*; *Three Wise Women*; *The Importance of Being Whatever* and *Primeval*.

Film credits include *The Lie of You*; *Tango One*; *The Doorway* and *The Pool*.

Seán Doyle | SEAN

Theatre credits include *Sive* (Druid); *Close to the Sun* (The Corps Ensemble); *Deadly* (Abbey Theatre); and *Boys and Girls* (Project Arts Centre and 59E59, New York).

Film and TV credits include *Metal Heart*; *Outside*; *Killing Bono* and *Fair City*.

Kwaku Fortune | ELI

Kwaku holds a Bachelor in Acting from The Lir Academy at Trinity College Dublin (in partnership with RADA).

Theatre credits include *On Raftery's Hill* (Abbey Theatre) and *Playboyz* (The New Theatre).

Film and TV credits include *Animals*, directed by Sophie Hyde; *Kissing Candice*; *Girl from Mogadishu*; *Circuit Love, Easy*; *Idle*; *Bible Studies*; *Tried and True*; *The Day after Yesterday*; *13 Steps Down* and *The Importance of Being Whatever*.

Síle Maguire | ALI

Síle is a recent graduate of Drama and Theatre Studies from Trinity College Dublin.

Recent theatre credits include *Everything can be Dismantled* (Dublin Fringe Festival); *The Maids*, *The World We Live In* and *For Every Atom Belonging to Me* (Samuel Beckett Theatre); *The Tempest* (ATRL Building, Trinity College); *The Children* (Jerome Hynes Theatre); and *True Confessions* (Wexford Arts Centre).

Charlie Maher | PAUL

Recent theatre credits include Rough Magic's production of *Melt* in Smock Alley as part of the Dublin Theatre Festival.

Recent TV and film credits include *Genius – Picasso: Chapter One* (Fox 21 Studios) and *Animals,* directed by Sophie Hyde.

Charlie is a graduate of The Lir. During his time at the Lir he appeared in *Three Winters*, *Children of the Sun*, *The Skriker*, *Much Ado About Nothing* and *Each Day Dies With Sleep*. Charlie also appeared in the short film *Dead Leaf Moth*, directed by Louise Ní Fhiannachta.

Frank McCusker | DAD

Abbey Theatre credits include *The Wake, The Picture of Dorian Gray, The Last Days of a Reluctant Tyrant, Romeo and Juliet, Julius Caesar, Defender of the Faith* (winner, Irish Times Irish Theatre Award for Best Supporting Actor), *The Wild Duck, Communion, The Sanctuary Lamp, Translations, The House, The Tempest, The Importance of Being Earnest, She Stoops to Folly, As the Beast Sleeps, Observe the Sons of Ulster Marching Towards the Somme, The Last Apache Reunion, The Gentle Island, The Lower Depths, The Playboy of the Western World* (Helen Hayes Award, Washington DC) and *The Glass Menagerie.*

Other theatre includes *The Ugly One* (Royal Court); *Under the Black Flag* and *Coriolanus* (Globe Theatre); *The Lonesome West* (Lyric, Belfast); *The Shadow of a Gunman* (Tricycle); *Aristocrats, The Collection* (Gate Theatre and Lincoln Center, New York); *Life Support* (Aldwych Theatre); *Wild Harvest* (Druid); *Moonshine* (Red Kettle); *Hamlet* and *King Lear* (Second Age); *Richard II* (Ouroboros); *Lally the Scut* (Tinderbox); *The Waste Land, Catastrophe* (Beckett Festival 2015); and *Wild Harvest* (Gaiety Theatre).

Television/film appearances include *Penny Dreadful, The Tudors, Titanic: Blood and Steel, 1916: Seachtar Dearmadta, The Frankenstein Chronicles, The Fall, My Mother and Other Strangers, Agnes Browne, David Copperfield, The Blackwater Lightship, Proof, Rebel Heart, Pulling Moves, As the Beast Sleeps, Out of Hours, Getting Hurt, The Railway Station Man, The Affair of the Necklace, Anytime Now, Murder Prevention, Bad Girls, Hunger* and others.

Amy McElhatton | MAGGIE

Amy is a graduate of The Lir, the National Academy of Dramatic Art.

Theatre credits include *The Lonesome West* (The Everyman); *Crestfall* (Druid); *The Sin Eaters* (ANU); *All's Well That Ends Well, The Skriker, Three Winters, Children of the Sun* (The Lir) and *Our Country's Good* (Lyric Theatre, Belfast).

Paul Mescal | BRYAN

Paul trained at the The Lir.

Theatre credits include *A Portrait of the Artist as a Young Man* and *A Midsummer Night's Dream* (Rough Magic); *The Plough and the Stars* (Lyric Hammersmith / Gaiety Theatre); *The Great Gatsby* and *The Red Shoes* (Gate Theatre, Dublin).

Film and TV credits include *Happish*, directed by Juanita Wilson.

Darragh Shannon | DYLAN

Darragh graduated from Kinsale College with a FETAC Level 5 in Drama Theatre Studies, and FETAC Level 6 in Classical Acting. He then went on to get a First Class Honours in Acting at The Lir Academy.

His Lir credits include *Three Winters*, *Children of The Sun*, *Mojo*, *All's Well that Ends Well* and *Dead Man's Cellphone*.

Other theatre credits include *Two of Clubs* (Theatre Upstairs); *Swansong* (Kilkenny Arts Festival); and *As You Like It* (Cork Arts Theatre).

Ali White | MAM

Recent theatre credits include *Roman Fever* (Bewley's Café Theatre); *Asking for It* (Landmark and The Everyman); *Fire Below* (Lyric Theatre Belfast); *The Effect*, *Northern Star* (winner, Irish Times Irish Theatre Award for Best Supporting Actress) and *Plaza Suite* (Rough Magic); *Lippy* (Dead Centre); *Bailed Out!* and *Guaranteed!* (Fishamble); *Deadly* and *Major Barbara* (Abbey Theatre); *God of Carnage* (Prime Cut); *Borstal Boy* (Gaiety Theatre); *This is What We Sang* (Kabosh) and *Faith Healer* (Town Hall Theatre Galway).

Other theatre work includes *The Picture of Dorian Gray*, *The Passing*, *Romeo and Juliet*, *Doldrum Bay*, *The House*, *Closer*, *Dancing at Lughnasa*, *Translations* and *Trojan Women* (Abbey Theatre); *Spokesong*, *Is This About Sex*, *School for Scandal*, *Lady Windermere's Fan* and *Love and a Bottle* (Rough Magic); *Benefactors* (b*spoke); *Love and Money* (Hatch Theatre Company); *Catastrophe*, *Come and Go*, *Play*, *A Midsummer Night's Dream*, *The Double Dealer* and *Aristocrats* (Gate Theatre); *The Importance of Being Earnest* and *All Soul's Night* (Lyric Theatre); *Playhouse Creatures* (The Old Vic); *The Silver Tassie* (Almeida); *The Importance of Being Earnest* (West Yorkshire Playhouse); *The Steward of Christendom* (Out of Joint at the Royal Court, BAM New York and Australian tour).

Film and TV work includes *The Bailout*; *Cellar Door*; *The Fall*; *The Secret*; *The Truth Commissioner*; *My Name is Emily*; *Fifty Dead Men Walking*; *No Tears*; *A Love Divided*; *With or Without You*; and *When Brendan met Trudy*.

Writing credits include *Any Time Now* (BBC/RTÉ); *The Clinic* (Parallel/RTÉ); *Catching the Fly* (BBC R4) and *Me, Mollser* (Abbey Theatre Community and Education Department).

ASKING FOR IT

Louise O'Neill

Adapted by Meadhbh McHugh
in collaboration with Annabelle Comyn

Characters

EMMA
ZOE
MAGGIE
ALI
CONOR
DYLAN
SEAN
ELI
PAUL
BRYAN
MAM
DAD

Note on Text

The script uses incomplete, broken, interrupted, discontinuous and non-consecutive dialogue, e.g. 'Ah. She's… treatment ends next week, so.'

Dialogue in brackets doesn't need to be said, but can be.

A blank line of dialogue means attention switches to the attributed character, although nothing is said.

A forward slash (/) means the next line of dialogue begins, and there is a brief overlap.

This text went to press before the end of rehearsals and so may differ slightly from the play as performed.

Prologue

EMMA, *the present*.

EMMA. I look at my reflection in the vanity mirror. How is it that two eyes, a nose and a mouth can be positioned in such varying ways that it makes one person beautiful, and another person not? What if my eyes had been a fraction closer together? Or if my nose had been flatter? My lips thinner, or my mouth too wide? Would my life have been different?

I close my eyes, and imagine a slash of a hook across my skin, scraping away this thing they call beauty, making me new. I blink, but it's only me.

(*Turns to the audience*.) I don't have anything to say, but you want to hear from me anyway. Everyone wants me to tell my story. I don't have a story.

When you can't remember something – and I can't remember, I have said so many times I can't remember – it is as if it never happened at all.

As she moves to sit down for Scene One.

'It's not your fault,' the therapist tells me. She is wrong. Hasn't she heard what everyone else has to say? 'No, it's not my fault,' I repeat after her. But I am lying. It was my fault. My fault, my fault, my fault, my fault.

EMMA *wraps herself in a dressing gown, and sits in her room to study. Morning light.*

ACT ONE

LAST YEAR

Scene One

One year previous.

MAM *is standing in* EMMA*'s bedroom. She has a dress on, which is perhaps unzipped at the top.*

MAM. Verdict?

EMMA. On what?

MAM. This dress.

EMMA. First thing in the morning?

MAM. I have to return it today if I'm not keeping it.

   What do you think?

   Beat.

EMMA. I'm busy.

MAM. You know I value your opinion.

EMMA. You walked straight in.

MAM. I knocked and waited for a response.

   You didn't respond.

EMMA (*looks up quickly and looks back down*). It's grand.

MAM. Grand?

EMMA. It's nice.

MAM. I'd like to look more than *nice* for our anniversary.

EMMA. What do you want me to say? It's *stunning*.

MAM. Alright. I thought you liked it in the shop.

EMMA. It's a bit short.

MAM. Is it?

EMMA. A bit, yeah.

MAM. I didn't think so.

EMMA. Why did you ask me if it you don't care what I actually think?

MAM. No, I just didn't think it was that short.

I'll see what Dad says.

EMMA. Right.

Beat.

MAM. Why so serious, love?

You know what they say

If the wind changes.

EMMA. I'm trying to understand Irish grammar.

I don't know how to do that without contorting my face.

MAM. Don't want to look old before your time.

EMMA. Blame our national language.

Beat.

We have a test today.

MAM. Does O'Leary know you're my daughter?

EMMA. He's not going to give me an A because he once fancied you.

MAM. We'll see.

EMMA *goes back to her work. Maybe picks up her phone and puts it back down with some frustration.*

I've barely seen you the last few weeks.

EMMA. You see me every day.

MAM. You know what I mean.

EMMA. I don't.

MAM. Okay, maybe I'll return it.

EMMA. No, keep it.

With frustration looks at phone.

My phone keeps glitching.

It dies now even when it's charged.

MAM (*they've had this conversation before*). Emma.

EMMA. Even Zoe Murphy has the new iPhone.

MAM. That's great for Zoe Murphy.

EMMA. And they're still bankrupt.

MAM. I don't compare our family to other families.

EMMA. Yes you do. You do that constantly.

MAM. I told you if Dad's upgrade comes through –

EMMA. I don't want Dad's old Samsung.

MAM. Then you'll have to wait until you're earning your own money.

EMMA. Fine. Then please let me study.

MAM. I will let you study.

EMMA. Okay.

I thought you were going down to ask Dad.

MAM. You'll stress yourself out, Emma. There's more to life than…

EMMA. School?

MAM. Is there something the matter with you lately?

EMMA (*to audience*). She will go downstairs and tell Dad, tell him I've been disrespectful and rude. He'll sigh and tell me that he is disappointed in me. He won't listen to me, no matter what I tell him, no matter how hard I explain. *There are no sides*, he'll say. *Please treat your mother with more respect.* That's not true. There are many sides and it is never mine.

MAM. Emma?

EMMA. No. Sorry.

MAM. Have you had a fallout with someone?

Pause. EMMA *shakes her head.*

EMMA. People don't fall out with me.

An ndeir tú? Deirim/Ní deirim.

An ndúirt tú? Dúirt/Ní dúirt.

MAM. When you're finished that, come downstairs to join Dad
and me for breakfast; he likes to see you before he leaves.

EMMA. An ndéarfaidh tú? Déarfaidh/Ní déarfaidh.

MAM. Smile, love.

You look beautiful this morning, Emma.

MAM *leaves.*

A moment.

EMMA *then puts on her school uniform and gets ready to go
to school. The world starts to appear.*

ZOE. 'They say if you put a frog in water and you slowly raise
the temperature, gradually, over time, the frog doesn't
register the changes, and it dies. You put it in water and you
suddenly raise the temperature, it bolts and it might survive.

Change, of any kind, is very stressful. Change can be
incremental or it can be sudden. Sudden change is a shock to
the system, and we have to adapt. Incremental change
happens all around us, and sometimes we don't even notice
it. That's what's happening with the earth's temperature now.
The planet is heating up, and most of us aren't registering it.
The changes, if they come as scientists predict they will, will
be disastrous if we don't stop to look around us, see what's
happening and make plans to make the world safer and better
for everyone.

But we don't like to face this idea, because it will mean
changing our behaviour, so we bury our heads in the sand. It's

better there. At least we think so now. What will our grandkids say about those of us who do nothing? Will they think we are selfish for prioritising our comfort now, over the truth?'

CONOR *appears as if he's waiting outside his house for a lift and waves at* EMMA.

CONOR. Emmie!

She doesn't turn until he does it again.

Hey, Emma O'Donovan!

EMMA *turns and waves and continues to the next scene.*

EMMA. That's my name, don't wear it out.

(*To audience.*) Conor Callaghan, neighbour, family friend, the man I should marry and grow old with. But I don't want to get married. My mother thinks I'll grow out of that 'notion', too.

ZOE. 'If we don't acknowledge what is happening around us and take action, then we, like the oblivious frog, are going to get massively burned.'

Scene Two

I

The bell goes.

ALI. Would you rather!

MAGGIE. Great presentation, Zo.

EMMA. Yeah, good use of *hyperbole.*

ALI. Hyper-bowl.

EMMA *and* MAGGIE *laugh,* ALI *is pleased.*

ZOE. It's science. They were facts.

ALI. Okay, would you rather be pretty or be smart?

EMMA. Pretty.

ALI. Yeah pretty. Life is easier.

ZOE (*to* EMMA). Ignorance is bliss?

I'd rather be smart, make heaps of money, and buy a new face if I had to.

MAGGIE. Also looks fade. I'd rather be able to have a conversation when I'm older, and enjoy a book.

EMMA. Snore. Thinking too much is bad for you. Gives you wrinkles. I'd rather be totally gorgeous and totally dumb.

MAGGIE. No you wouldn't really.

EMMA. I would. Like a trophy wife. That's my aspiration in life. Like your mom, Ali.

ALI. Hey!

EMMA (*to audience*). I got seventy-eight per cent in a physics test last week. Mr O'Flynn, the teacher, winked and murmured *Well Done*. I left it on my desk so everyone could see it. *Then in first place*, he announced, *congratulations, Zoe*. Ninety-three per cent scrawled across the front in red marker. Her expression didn't change. It was as if the number drifted off the page, came towards me and seared itself into my eyes. I wanted to rip it into a thousand pieces.

(*To the girls*.) That's a boring dilemma anyhow.

What about a permanent penis on your back, or vagina on your forehead?

MAGGIE. Oh my god, girl.

ALI. Definitely dick on back. Sure it'd just be the same as getting the 108 Bus into Cork city.

They all laugh.

The action fades/slows as MAGGIE *speaks*.

MAGGIE (*to audience*). I believe that friendship is a relationship like any other and I believe in loyalty, which Emma *has*, and that you get out what you put in, which I *do*, but...

The bell goes for class.

We see some of the boys on stage, messing around, throwing a pack of crisps or a sandwich.

II

The bell goes for lunch, they eat.

ALI. Your sandwich looks so good.

MAGGIE. It's just ham.

Beat. ALI *stares.*

Do you want a bite?

ALI. I'm doing intermittent fasting.

Beat.

I might faint.

EMMA. How long have you been fasting?

ALI. An hour.

EMMA *laughs and is about to say something.*

ZOE. Okay, fat for ever, or lose a finger?

ALI. Which hand?

ZOE. Why does that matter?

ALI. If you were right-handed...

ZOE. Yeah, you could be trained to be left-handed.

MAGGIE. They used to do that the other way around.

My dad was a citeog and they made him be the other one. Write the right way. Sort of abusive.

It's weird, like, what we think was okay to do back then. You know they say in a hundred years we're going to look at eating meat in the same way we understand slavery now?

ALI. Really?

MAGGIE. I read that. We're going to have a different understanding of animals and look back and be shocked by how morally blind we were.

EMMA. Please don't use phrases like 'morally blind'.

MAGGIE. Why not?

EMMA. Cos you sound like a loser.

I'm a vegetarian anyhow so no one will say I was morally blind.

ZOE. No, just attention-seeking. You always eat meat when you're drunk.

ALI. I'd rather lose a finger.

MAGGIE. Maybe you'd be happy being… fuller and fully fingered. You could be a pianist, or a painter or a plus-size hand model.

EMMA. Maggie, stop being mature. You're ruining the game.

MAGGIE. I'm not mature. I'm just *saying*.

ZOE. Fully fingered is a really gross phrase.

EMMA. Do you think Eli would be with you if you were, like, Ten-Ton-Tessie?

MAGGIE. I do. Not everything is superficial.

EMMA. Sexual attraction is superficial?

MAGGIE. No, but I heard that overweight people are the best in bed.

EMMA. You wouldn't worry about him copping off with someone else?

Beat.

(*Dismissive.*) Depends on what you're into, I guess. What kind of fetishes you have.

Beat. MAGGIE *rolls her eyes.*

MAGGIE. God, it's so hot.

EMMA. Sure we're all going to fry, aren't we, Zo?

ALI. Snapchat story.

EMMA. Act like we like each other, girls.

MAGGIE. We do!

They laugh and pose for a selfie. EMMA *puts her arms around the girls and beams.*

ALI (*to audience*). Emma stole a pair of Warby Parker sunglasses Dad got me last year, and she thinks I don't know but they're a square shape and brown animal print that you can only get in America. Being friends with Emma is a bit like being lady-in-waiting to the queen, but I guess it's a trade-off having second-hand status, isn't it? You get some of the nice perks, but your head is rarely on the chopping block.

SEAN *appears upstage carrying a ball.*

ALI. Oh my god, Sean Casey looked at me. I think he just made love to me with his eyes.

He stops and sees ALI.

Hi, Sean.

SEAN *raises his hand and continues on.*

Good luck in the match!

III

MAGGIE. Who's driving to the match tomorrow?

ALI. I will!

EMMA. Okay I have one. Would you rather give an STD, or get one?

ZOE. Ugh.

ALI. Get one.

If you give one, you have one anyhow, and then you have to deal with the shame of other people knowing.

EMMA. I think I'd rather have symptomless chlamydia than a bad yeast infection, seriously.

MAGGIE. It's not actually funny. STDs are dangerous.

EMMA. You know what else is dangerous?

MAGGIE. What?

EMMA. Being up there on your high horse.

EMMA jumps on ALI*'s shoulders shouting 'You're all morally blind!'* MAGGIE *laughs.*

ZOE. You talking from experience, Ems? Chlamydia?

EMMA. No.

ZOE. Oh.

EMMA. Hey, Zoe, watch it.

ZOE. You're just so good at keeping things quiet.

Beat.

EMMA. If it makes life easier for everyone, yeah.

ZOE. For everyone else. Yeah.

EMMA (*to* ZOE). Do you have something to say, Zo?

If you do, just say it straight out.

Beat.

They stare at each other. All stare at ZOE, *to see if she'll speak.*

ZOE (*to audience*). What if there's a nuclear war, what if there's a terrorist attack in Cork, what if I sleepwalk out my window and die from exposure and get eaten by my dog and then my family shoot the dog and my brother resents me even in my death. What if I don't get into college, what if I *do* get into college and I can't get out of bed in the morning and I fail or I never make any friends, or they think I'm weird, and then I isolate myself and never have any support system which is actually my fault anyhow. What if I try REALLY hard to do everything right and I succeed, I succeed in every possible way and then I wake up when I'm forty and I realise I did everything wrong, that at every step of the way there was something else I should have done and it is *glaringly* obvious, like *screamingly* obvious to everyone and it always was but I didn't do it because I genuinely can't hear or see the signs and I don't know how to make the right moves. Or even how to move. That I was waiting for some kind of permission to move and then I realise that it's never going to come, that I can only give that to myself and then it's too late. That's what I think about. I mean, clearly Emma knows I'm depressed. What does she want me to say here in front of everyone? Bitch.

The bell goes again.

ZOE. I have to go study for this Irish test.

EMMA. Oh god, I completely forgot about that.

Scene Three

DYLAN *smokes*. SEAN, ELI *and* CONOR *hang around him*.

SEAN. Yeah but if Badger wasn't off in Sydney, we'd have that sorted.

I'm just concerned that our backs are dodgy with Mitch in there instead.

ELI. Dodgy? Mitch is solid.

SEAN. Yeah?

CONOR. Ballinatoom are really fit right now too.

I see Paul O'Brien every night in the gym.

ELI. Doesn't Paul O'Brien own the gym?

DYLAN. And every other fucking thing in town.

CONOR. Well, his dad.

ELI. Ciaran O'Brien: King of Ballinatoom. Fair play to him.

DYLAN. Fucking hell.

SEAN. Yeah we're fit alright. (*To* CONOR, *slightly dismissive*.) What do you do in the gym?

ELI. Have you seen Badger's Instagram? A lot of birds, by the looks of it.

DYLAN. Fucking hell. Fucking Badger, cleaning up.

SEAN. Did he have to go all the way to Oz to get his hole though?

Could he not have thought of the team, the town?

Plenty of class ladies in Ballinatoom.

DYLAN. Girls are better looking down under anyhow, pardon the pun.

ELI. Yeah, how so?

DYLAN. None of this fake-tan, fake-eyelashes shit.

Unless it's one of your sisters now, Eli. That'd be different. No need for fake tan on those beauties.

ELI. Don't even fucking joke, Dylan. I'll point you so far in the other direction.

DYLAN. I know you would, man. Jokes. Chill.

He laughs. ELI *sort of does.*

ELI. God, you're thick.

DYLAN (*to* ELI, *hitting him on the arm*). Jokes, man.

ELI. I know, lad. But if you touch my sisters.

ELI *hits* DYLAN *back a bit harder but still playfully.*

They really laugh this time. DYLAN *surrenders.*

CONOR. He'll disfigure you.

DYLAN (*serious tone, suddenly, to* CONOR). He'll what?

No one laughs.

SEAN. Someone told me once the sky in Australia is much bigger than here. Like the size of the planet seems bigger when you can see all that blue.

DYLAN (*sarcasm*). That's beautiful. Can I use that line at the weekend?

CONOR. Sean, you were saying. The match.

SEAN. That's how I predict the match'll go anyhow.

Not that I'm not shitting myself.

ELI. Are you not always shitting yourself, Seaneen Óg?

ELI ruffles SEAN's hair playfully.

DYLAN. Did you not shit yourself during – (*Makes sex gestures.*) one time?

The lads laugh.

SEAN. Fuck off, Dylan.

DYLAN keeps miming. He grabs SEAN and thrusts at him from behind. Lads laugh.

What are ya even talking about? (*Trying to laugh.*) Get off me.

CONOR. In Sean's defence, I never heard that.

SEAN. That's not saying a lot. You haven't heard of much.

The lads laugh. CONOR blushes.

DYLAN. It's all ahead of you, Conor.

CONOR. Thanks, Dylan. If you say so.

I have to go to class.

DYLAN. You'll be pumping drunk girls yet.

CONOR goes.

ELI. Same.

He leaves.

DYLAN. Yiz are all as dry as my granny's –

He stops short of the punchline.

What was I gonna say, Sean?

SEAN. Hole.

DYLAN. You dirty-minded bastard! I was going to say eyes. She's got dry eyes.

DYLAN *laughs*.

SEAN. Girlfriend trouble, what?

DYLAN. No. Who said that?

SEAN (*conceding a bit*). Dunno. Just.

You're on edge, or something.

SEAN *starts to leave*.

DYLAN. What about you and that Asian one. She's gagging for it.

SEAN. Yeah?

DYLAN. Have you seen her mother?

Absolute ride.

I'd bang her in a heartbeat. Bang them both. (*As he makes sexual gestures*.) A mother-daughter, spicy hot bag, three-in-one.

Fuck I'm at half-mast just thinking about it.

Beat.

Get on it, boy.

SEAN. I know, I know, I will.

Need to stay focused on the game, though.

DYLAN. Why?

SEAN. Just. It's a big one.

DYLAN. Selectors coming?

Your priorities are fucked up. The county people won't kneel at the altar, will they? Get a few more notches on the post that matters, mate.

SEAN. I have notches.

DYLAN *looks at him skeptically.*

I fucking have…

Piss off.

DYLAN. Wouldn't mind going to Oz myself someday.

Get away from the missus before she has me caught with two babas and a mortgage around my balls.

(*Sees* SEAN *is pissed.*) I'm only messin' with ya, Seaneen. You're becoming neurotic now like your mam.

SEAN. That's fucking you that's neurotic.

DYLAN. Is it not around this time she gets the looniest?

Beat.

SEAN. The anniversary, yeah.

DYLAN (*sort of casually*). Poor John Junior. I often think of him in the slurry pit.

It's a terrible image, isn't it? Your brother drowning in all that mud. I often think of it.

Your ma gone away again for it?

SEAN. Jen is sending them to a hotel in Killarney.

To care would we face it.

DYLAN. Old man too?

SEAN *nods.*

Free gaff then…? Every cloud. And all that.

Pause.

I'm not going to accounting, are you?

Beat.

SEAN. Well, what's your take on the game, then?

(*Almost desperately.*) I really fucking hope we win this match.

DYLAN. I don't give a fuck whether ye win or not.

Scene Four

EMMA. Who wants one of my mam's muffins?

    ALI *salivates*.

    (*To audience*.) I can't help myself.

    (*To* ALI.) Oh, sorry, Ali. I forgot about your diet.

    And Zoe doesn't eat muffins, either.

    More for you and me, Mags.

ZOE. What the fuck? Have you ever seen me not eat one? Give me one right now and I'll eat it.

    EMMA *gives her a muffin*.

EMMA (*to audience*). Just to have something, anything, happen.

    ZOE *stuffs it into her mouth*.

ALI. Okay I'll have one, too.

    EMMA *smiles*.

    ALI *grabs one and turns*.

    Don't look now, but three o'clock, boys are coming.

    All girls look right.

    CONOR *arrives*.

CONOR. Emmie!

    Sorry, Emma.

    SEAN, DYLAN *and* ELI *appear, filling out the stage. They throw sun cream around, or take* EMMA*'s from her and pass it around. She squeals, etc*.

EMMA (*to audience*). Dylan arrives in the park with the lads. He doesn't even look at me, just stares at Zoe. *Emma O'Donovan is hot*, I overheard a boy say when I was fourteen and going to the Attic Disco, *but she's as boring as fuck*.

ZOE *is awkward.*

DYLAN. I said 'Hello Zoe', no need to be ignorant.

MAGGIE. Take a hint, Dylan.

She hugs ELI.

DYLAN. Someone ask you, lovebird?

ELI. Hey, man, don't speak to my girlfriend like that.

MAGGIE *pulls him away.*

DYLAN. Whipped!

ELI. Thick!

DYLAN *laughs.*

They disappear.

DYLAN (*to* ZOE). In or out for tomorrow night? Sean has a free gaff. The man needs definitive answers.

EMMA. If we don't get any better offers.

DYLAN. Can't handle the sesh, O'Donovan?

EMMA *laughs.*

EMMA. Yes I can.

SEAN (*to audience*). Emma O'Donovan wins Ballinatoom Queen at the football gala last year, which I bring her to, and her face is up on a billboard outside town. Every man in the town fantasising about her that month.

I take a sneaky photo of it and keep it in the wank bank, so to speak. Her lips, man I fixate on her lips, and I still do when I see her, they're just perfect like roses, no like rosebuds, I almost come in my pants thinking about them. I wrote her a card once as a child and it said: 'If I was a dog and you were a flower, I'd lift up my leg and give you a shower.'

(*Back to group.*) Ah, she can hold a few vodka Red Bulls.

ALI. We all can, actually, Sean.

DYLAN. You had a good time at my last party, didn't you?

EMMA. It was okay.

SEAN. Fucking hell, it's hot.

DYLAN (*to* EMMA). That's not what I heard. Yourself and Zoe went down a storm.

CONOR (*diverting*). Hottest temperature on record they're saying.

EMMA (*ignoring* CONOR*'s attempt at diversion*). What did you hear?

DYLAN. Just that you had fun.

EMMA. What kind of fun?

SEAN (*under breath in a cough*). Kevin Brennan.

DYLAN *laughs,* SEAN *follows.*

EMMA. Nothing happened with Kevin Brennan.

DYLAN. That's not what I've been told.

EMMA. If people have to make up stories to make themselves feel more like men that's not my problem.

ZOE *goes to leave. Her pencil case might drop.* ALI *gets up with her. They pick up her things.*

DYLAN. And if women have to make up stories to make themselves feel better about themselves, it's not mine.

CONOR. Jesus, Dylan. If she said (nothing happened) –

EMMA. Yeah, alright, Conor.

DYLAN *directs the following at* ZOE. *Or he gets in her way.*

DYLAN. Girls are all the same, aren't they, Zoe? Get wasted, get a bit slutty, then in the morning you try and pretend it never happened because you regret it.

EMMA *laughs.* SEAN *might too.*

Emma agrees. She concedes to Mr Walsh.

What do you reckon, Zo?

ZOE *doesn't say anything as she stands up.*

ZOE. I have to get to work.

She goes to leave. ALI *follows.*

DYLAN. No need to run off. Sean.

The boys leave. ALI *waits at the edge.*

EMMA (*to* ZOE). What?

CONOR (*to audience*). I find a photo this week, of me and
    Emma as kids, where our parents dress us up and have this,
    like, mock-wedding for us with confetti and cake while they
    sit around drinking wine. She has this little white dress on
    and is carrying a huge bouquet of flowers and I have an old
    top hat of my dad's that covers almost my whole face apart
    from my toothless smile. Emma's got her arm around me,
    she's taller than me, and she's looking very seriously at the
    camera like she's the one in charge.

    Emma doesn't like anyone to come up too close.

    She always likes to be in control.

    Mum hands me the photo as if to say *get on it*. I don't send
    the photo to Emma, though. I wait.

    EMMA *looks at* ZOE.

EMMA. Sense of humour. Dylan really fancies you.

ZOE. He doesn't know me. I have to go.

EMMA. What did you get in your chemistry?

ZOE. A2.

EMMA. Me too.

Beat.

Come on. We… agreed it was best not to…

ZOE *stares at her.*

ZOE. I really have to get to work.

ZOE *exits.*

EMMA (*calling after her*). See you at Sean's!

CONOR *and* EMMA *are left.*

Slightly awkward moment. EMMA *is a bit distracted.*

CONOR. I thought I'd wait.

EMMA. Oh. Thanks.

She might give him a friendly punch on the arm.

CONOR. It's nice to see you.

Thanks again for… coming around last week. Mam loved the headscarf.

EMMA *waves the thanks away. Maybe she squeezes his arm.*

EMMA. How is she?

CONOR. Ah. She's… treatment ends next week, so.

Sorry again about getting a bit…

EMMA. It was fine, Conor. You were upset. Don't apologise.

CONOR. But I am grateful to you.

(*Touches her arm and their eyes lock.*) Look at me, I mean that.

EMMA (*looks away*). Don't mention it.

(*To audience.*) I feel something melting in me and it's something I have to shut down and control. I peer into the houses as we drive home, in one semi-detached a middle-aged couple sit with glasses of wine in their hands, clinging to opposite ends of the sofa in case they would accidentally touch. My gaze drifts across all the houses in the estate, chairs and faces focused on the TV. Same same same. I imagine squeezing the wine glass until it breaks in my hand.

CONOR. But here, why did you laugh?

EMMA. What?

CONOR. Earlier. When Dylan said that about Zoe.

EMMA. It was just a joke.

CONOR. Zoe seemed upset. Didn't something happen with her and Dylan? You shouldn't have laughed.

EMMA. What do you care?

(*To audience.*) Her face again in my mind, stricken. Her coming to my house last month.

CONOR. You just seem a bit…

EMMA. Yeah?

CONOR. Uh.

EMMA. What?

CONOR. Not yourself?

EMMA. How would you know?

When's the last time we even properly hung out?

CONOR *looks a bit surprised*.

CONOR. I mean, not for lack of me trying.

Are you okay?

EMMA *realises she's being unattractive. Catches herself.*

EMMA. Yes, Conor. I'm wonderful. Don't be such an Anxious Annie.

Will you hold my bag for a minute?

He holds her bag and she takes off her jacket/jumper revealing her stomach, or takes down her hair seductively. She watches CONOR *watching her.*

(*Changes tone again.*) Maybe see you tomorrow night.

She leaves.

CONOR. Okay. See you… tomorrow night.

(*Calls after her.*) Are you going to the match?

He leaves.

We see EMMA *return home to find her room straightened out.*

Cheers for the match might start under this.

MAM. It was a mess.

EMMA. But, it's my mess.

MAM. I was trying to be nice.

EMMA. I'll ask if I want you to be nice.

MAM. You're going to be dissatisfied your whole life, Emma.

It was untidy and I cleaned it. End of.

EMMA has turned her face into pillow/phone.

EMMA. Would you wipe me away too if you could?

MAM. What's that?

EMMA *(with frustrated need)*. I just wish –

MAM. What do you wish?

If I grew up with half of what you have…

EMMA. A good daughter would be grateful.

Beat.

MAM. Yes.

And brush your hair, darling, please. If Dad sees you looking like that, he'll wonder what I'm doing with you at all. Who'll have you looking like that?

EMMA balks.

Lighten up, I'm hardly serious.

EMMA *(to audience, exasperated)*. Gahhh…

The heat feels like it's pressing down on me, like it might make an imprint on my skin. I wonder what it would feel like to be flattened into the earth and be discovered centuries in the future as a fossil. Who would they think I was? What would they say I was? Would they… understand? I lie on my bed for hours.

Ballinatoom cheers. 'C'mon Ballinatoom!'

The girls pose around EMMA, who has not moved. Capture.

ALI. 'Me and my girls, Fresh as fuck.'

EMMA (*to audience*). Ali quickly tags us in a photo on Instagram at the match, a selfie of the four of us.

MAGGIE. You could be a model, Zoe.

EMMA (*to audience*). I look at the photo closely. I'm definitely the prettiest out of us four.

ALI. C'mon Ballinatoom! Move your asses.

We hear shouts from the match. 'Fucking open your eyes','Get your shit together Ballinatoom', etc.

MAM. What are your plans for tonight?

We hear cheers and screams continue. A goal. A whistle blowing.

EMMA (*to audience*). Paul O'Brien looks at me with intent when leaving the pitch. I pull my top down to reveal a bit more, and my legs tremble with so much adrenalin I think I might actually be sick.

MAM. Emma?

EMMA (*to* MAM). Nothing much, a DVD in Maggie's or something.

MAM. And who will be there?

EMMA. The girls. Maybe Eli, and Conor.

MAM. Okay. Well… Bryan's in charge.

EMMA (*to audience*). Her voice a little cool as Dad puts the last of their overnight bags in the car. I'm eighteen, I'm an adult, what does it matter what I do?

MAM. Call me at midnight, from the house phone.

Beat.

See you tomorrow.

EMMA (*to audience*). And their car pulls out. *Freedom.* I am Emma O'Donovan, it's Saturday night and Ballinatoom win.

More cheers for Ballinatoom to win.

PAUL *lights up*.

PAUL *speaks to a reporter either on camera or tape*.

PAUL (*smiles*). Absolutely delighted with the result today.
Great game, great bunch of lads, the whole community came
out for us today and we showed our true colours out on the
pitch. They had our backs against the wall earlier in the
second half, but we really put the shoulder to the wheel.
Proud of all the lads on the pitch today. Ah yeah, there'll be
a few beers tonight alright.

Thanks now. Thanks.

PAUL *waves to the fans*.

He could raise a cup.

Tá áthas an domhain orm an corn seo a ghlacadh ar son
foireann Baile na Tuaime.

Wild cheers.

Cameras flash at him.

SEAN. We did it! We fucking did it!

Lad, I love ye!

The girls are there.

Ye'll come to the house now.

EMMA. Is that a question or a statement?

DYLAN. You tell us.

ALI. You played a blinder, Sean.

DYLAN *might nudge him in* ALI's *direction, and laugh*.

ELI. Good man, Seaneen.

SEAN. What do you think, Emma?

EMMA (*teasingly*). You played well… the half that you
were on.

DYLAN. Spicy.

(*With a crude hand gesture*.) He's a handy player all the same. Even for a sub.

MAGGIE. So gross.

MAGGIE *looks at* ZOE *to see her reaction*.

EMMA (*innuendo*). We better come tonight, so.

ALI *looks at* EMMA.

(*Conceding a little*.) Hah, Al?

ALI.... Yeah.

Yeah, we'll be there.

ZOE *looks on silently*.

EMMA. The question is, are the real men going to show?

DYLAN. Oi – speaking of – look who it is, Emma.

CONOR *enters*.

EMMA *turns expectantly*.

EMMA (*to audience*). I spin too quickly on my heels.

But it's only him.

EMMA *gives* DYLAN *a look, and* DYLAN *laughs*.

CONOR *gives* SEAN *a hug*.

CONOR. Casey! Didn't know you had that in you.

SEAN (*laughing*). All you fuckers doubted me.

Come at me, come at me.

CONOR *charges at him playfully. Back-slapping, etc*.

CONOR *brings the girls*, ALI *and* EMMA, *into a bear hug with* SEAN, *too*.

ELI *grabs* MAGGIE. *They laugh*.

ELI. Ballinatoom hi hi hi! (*Or some kind of chant*.)

Others join in chant.

ZOE stands slightly apart. DYLAN watches her for a moment while stomping his feet to the rhythm. She disappears.

Music starts for dance.

Into a celebratory, rhythmic, sensual dance routine with boys and girls.

Music halts.

MAGGIE. Where's Zoe?

EMMA. LADS! Let's get this shit kicked off.

DYLAN. Cans, lads! The can man is here.

Who wants a can?

Can in the air. Heads over there.

No need to fear, the can man is here.

EMMA (*to* ALI). Never have I ever kissed a girl.

ALI doesn't drink. Looks offended.

MAGGIE. Has anyone seen Zoe?

EMMA (*to* ELI). Never have I ever sent nudes.

ELI drinks. MAGGIE hits him. He kisses MAGGIE.

(*To* CONOR.) Never have I ever fancied a friend.

CONOR drinks. A moment between them. He wants to kiss her. They might kiss. She pulls away.

Never would I –

ZOE appears at the party.

You're here.

ZOE. Did you think I wasn't going to show?

EMMA (*to audience*). I can smell a trace of vomit on her breath.

EMMA does an awkward greeting.

(*To* ZOE.) Are you wearing that?

Beat.

Do you want to borrow something from me?

ZOE. This is fine.

EMMA. It's just, you look like a...

ZOE. What?

EMMA. Some sort of a victim, Zo.

ZOE. Thanks.

You look like a fraud.

ZOE *knocks back a drink. Music starts again in background.*

EMMA (*to* ZOE). Never would I ever... squeal like a bitch.

ZOE *walks away.*

Music up.

ALI *orchestrates a type of group photo.*

ALI (*to audience*). I upload us with the boys. Boys add credibility, always. And we're on our way.

PAUL *enters with the lads chanting his name.* PAUL, *as hero, is on the boys' shoulders.*

ELI (*to audience*). Emma has her eyes on Paul the minute he arrives at the party.

EMMA (*to audience*). I see Paul arriving at the party. I pretend not to notice.

MAGGIE (*for his attention*). Eli?

ALI. Where's Sean?

ZOE *drinks.*

MAGGIE. Slow down, Zo.

ALI. How do I look?

ZOE *keeps drinking.*

Where's Sean?

EMMA *clinks glasses or has a moment with/passing*
DYLAN. ZOE *sees*.

ELI. BALLINATOOM HI HI HI!

DYLAN. Let's go fucking men-tal!

The lads cheer.

Choreography to show time passing.

DYLAN *watches* ZOE.

ZOE (*to audience*). A girl goes into a room with a guy and
I want to shout at her. I follow down the hallway and have to
stop myself from screaming at her as I press myself against
the back of the door. I am panicked at every door I see
closing. A girl trips on her high heel, and I imagine how easy
it would be to pounce on her. I hear the sounds of laughter
like knives on my spine. Dylan watches me all night as if
I'm prey, and when Emma presses up to him with her chest,
I break.

EMMA *is now standing with* PAUL.

(*To* EMMA.) What the fuck were you doing?

EMMA. Excuse me?

ZOE (*to* PAUL). Do you not have a fiancée?

EMMA. Sorry, Paul.

ZOE *shoves* EMMA.

Oh my god.

ZOE. This is all wrong.

PAUL *makes a gesture as if to say, 'I'll leave you to it.'*
Backs away.

EMMA. No, Paul.

He leaves.

That's the captain of the football team.

EMMA *shoves her back.*

ZOE. This is fucking hell with him here.

EMMA. Your make-up is all over the place.

ZOE. Emma, I'm gonna do something.

EMMA. Get sick if it'll help you.

EMMA *grabs* ZOE *by her hair and holds her head out in a position in which she could get sick.*

Do you even care? It's all down your cheek.

ZOE (*head down*). I have to say something about Dylan. I'm going to go to the –

EMMA (*pulls her up*). Look at yourself, your face is falling off.

You're letting the side down.

ZOE. I'm gonna go to the guards, I –

EMMA *laughs.*

What's funny?

EMMA. Are you going to call them drunk? Are you going to say, 'I'm at a party with him right now.'

ZOE. Not / right now.

EMMA. How much have you had to drink?

ZOE. What?

EMMA. You're a mess, Zo.

ZOE. You know it's the same thing with you and Kevin Brennan that night at Dylan's.

EMMA. It's not.

ZOE. I have texts from you that say something different.

EMMA. Okay, just / calm down.

ZOE. And I'll show them to the guards too.

EMMA. Calm the fuck down.

They are in a loo.

Zoe. Zoe. Look at me.

Look at me. We agreed.

You don't want to let a one-night stand take over your whole life.

ZOE. But it wasn't *that* –

EMMA. But I wasn't in the room with you. How can I honestly say?

ZOE. Because I *told* you.

EMMA. You told me you didn't say 'no'.

ZOE. I didn't say 'yes'.

EMMA. Okay but, we sat down and we agreed this was better, didn't we? Once you say that *word*, you can't take it back.

Everything we've worked for will be undone just like that. We risk *everything* if you say that word. It's all anyone will remember you by. This place is tiny, it's a tiny world. No more 'smart Zoe', or 'Zoe who's going for medicine', or 'Zoe with the gorgeous blue eyes'. It'll be 'Zoe who… had sex, regretted it and ruined a boy's life.'

Think of college, think of what's *ahead*. Don't think about Dylan-fuckin-Walsh.

ZOE. Yeah? I don't know.

EMMA. You're panicking now, and you're drunk, you can't think straight, but I'm right. I promise you I'm right on this.

ZOE. I don't know. I don't know –

EMMA. The alternative isn't better.

ZOE. Okay.

EMMA. There is no alternative.

Beat.

ZOE *might retch.*

I can't be in here.

EMMA *bolts*.

CONOR *comes and helps out*.

CONOR. She okay?

EMMA. Fine.

CONOR *might try to grab* EMMA.

EMMA *pushes* CONOR *away, and heads towards* PAUL, *she may pull him away or dance provocatively*.

CONOR (*to audience*). Christ, Emma. Who is this all for?

CONOR *helps* ZOE.

Choreography to show more time passing.

EMMA *breaks away*.

EMMA (*to audience*). I see that Paul and Dylan are doing drugs. I've never taken anything before, but tonight I'm going to take a pill. I want to understand that *word*, *ecstasy*. I heard that it feels like pure bliss, like floating in the sea or flying, like you are everything and nothing at the one time, *infinite*, and that everything makes *sense*, everything feels *right* as you're carried along on a wave of pure pleasure. And fuck it I want to feel pure bliss. I just. I want so badly to be infinite for one brief moment in time.

PAUL *is doing drugs. She flirts with him*.

(*To* PAUL, *over the music*.) What was that you gave Dylan?

PAUL. Nothing an innocent girl like you should be concerned with.

EMMA. Who says I'm innocent?

PAUL. Want one?

Beat. She might catch sight of CONOR *looking at her and her friends. She turns away*.

EMMA. Yeah I want it.

PAUL. You wouldn't tell anyone, now, would you?

EMMA. Wouldn't look good, captain of the football team.

He smirks. He holds the stuff away from her.

PAUL (*shouting over music*). Flirty. I saw you on that billboard outside town, after the football gala, last year.

EMMA. Oh yeah?

PAUL. You marched over here like you're on some kind of mission.

EMMA. Yeah I am.

PAUL. Confident.

EMMA. You going to give me one or not?

PAUL. What are you gonna give me in return?

EMMA. My gratitude.

PAUL. I'll want more than that, love.

EMMA. Paul, the thing is I know what I want.

And I wanna get out of this room.

PAUL. Metaphorically now, or literally?

EMMA. Both.

He smiles, he takes out a tablet from a small plastic bag and hands it to her, secretly, palm to palm.

EMMA *and* PAUL *disappear.*

Everyone dances/choreography to complete the party.

The party slows down as if the night is ending.

Unnerving sound as party disperses. EMMA *is nowhere to be seen.*

ELI. Let's get outta here.

MAGGIE. Is Emma with Conor?

ELI. I saw Conor leave with Zoe.

MAGGIE. Why Conor?

ALI. Emma asked him.

ELI. Such a manipulator.

MAGGIE. You were flirting with her tonight.

ELI. No I wasn't.

ALI. It did look like that, Eli.

ELI. Shut up, Ali.

ALI. Where's Sean?

I think Emma's with Paul O'Brien.

MAGGIE. *Paul O'Brien* Paul? He's ten years older.

ALI. *She* pulled him down the hall. She better be, if she's with Sean I will never speak to her again.

ALI *exits*.

MAGGIE. I said I'd go home with her.

ELI. There's some pills going around. Would she take one?

MAGGIE. I wouldn't have thought so, but.

ELI. Emma's a big girl. She knows what's she doing.

MAGGIE. I should wait.

ELI. She can fend for herself.

MAGGIE. Did she try to kiss you tonight?

Beat.

EMMA *lights up, alone*.

EMMA. Conor texts to see if he should come back but I don't respond. No one would be impressed by Conor.

I am rising now, coming up up UP, and I can feel it in my veins, in my bones, I have never felt so good, I feel *so good*.

Paul kisses me. 'Hi,' I say as we fall into Sean's parents' bedroom down the hall. 'Hi,' he says. He wants me, I can see it in his eyes, his pure seething desire writes itself across his face and it gives me *life*. I kiss him, a shiver running through me again, filling my empty bones as we kiss, filling me, filling me *up*. This is what I've craved, and I have craved. I have craved so much. To feel powerful, to feel like I'm *something*, *someone…*

Elsewhere.

MAGGIE. Did she, try to kiss you?

ELI.…I pulled away.

MAGGIE (*to* ELI). Okay. Let's go.

They leave.

EMMA. But I'm getting hot and my mouth is dry. I'm thirsty and I need some water. My mouth is so dry now and it feels like my lips are swelling up. I stop kissing Paul. I need water and his belt buckle is digging into my hip. I am so high right now. I stop as if to –

He takes his clothes off, he is naked, though we were just kissing. He is naked so fast. I am not naked. We were kissing. My lips swell.

He turns me around and the room spins. His hands on my hips feel good, he is strong, but

I am melting now and my mouth is so dry.

'Wait,' I say. 'Wait I don't feel…' but he's yanked my underwear down to my knees and my face is pushed flat sideways on a flower duvet and there's a rose eating my face.

'Maybe we should go back to the…' meaning party, I say, because I want to go back to my friends now, because I'm sorry I was an asshole, and I love Zoe I do, but he says not to be a cock-tease and he's suddenly inside me and I'm not ready and it hurts, and he's thrusting himself into me and telling me I'm a slut and that I want it, I know I want it.

I don't know, I don't know, I don't know if I want it, and is he wearing a condom? I should stop him and ask if he's wearing a condom, but he'll think I'm a slut if I say that, and he's in the middle of it now, and it's too late anyhow, it's too late, but they always say in magazines to carry condoms, oh god –

He pulls my hair, hard, and he bites my shoulder and it hurts, I moan, I make the moan bigger, I think they like that, and it'll end sooner, I moan again as he slams himself into my body over and over. Maybe it's supposed to feel like this. Do other girls like this?

It's too late now, and it doesn't matter, who cares anyhow, he's enjoying it I think and that's good I suppose isn't it, it means that I'm good, doesn't it?

I look at the photo of John Junior on the bed stand and I think of him in that slurry pit all those years ago and he can't breathe with his mouth crammed full of shit and I gasp as I beg him in some kind of pact to make it stop, for it to be over, and finally it is.

Long pause. EMMA *is shocked.*

We see PAUL *emerge from behind her.*

PAUL. Fuck that was amazing.

Did you come?

Beat.

EMMA. Hah? Yeah. Uh. Of course I did.

PAUL. You've got a little something on your back. A present.

Beat. EMMA *registers a mini-humiliation. He laughs.*

EMMA *moves forward as if in a bathroom on her own. She contorts her face and touches her skin as if looking into a mirror. As if to see if she's still there.*

EMMA. I am Emma O'Donovan, I am Emma O'Donovan, I am Emma O'Donovan.

A door opens.

Somewhere else on stage, DYLAN *and* SEAN *join* PAUL. EMMA *temporarily not visible.* SEAN *is falling around the place. He follows* DYLAN *into the room.*

DYLAN. Is this where the party's at?

SEAN. This is my parents' room, lads.

PAUL. Shut the door.

Come out here, Emma, and show the lads your nice ass.

SEAN. Olé olé olé olé!

PAUL. Close the door.

SEAN. Is there another party happening? Let's get outta here. This is my parents' room.

PAUL. There is, let me get the address.

Does anyone have any stuff?

SEAN. My mam has some stuff, in the bathroom.

PAUL. Perfect.

DYLAN. Horse tranquiliser, is it?

SEAN (*hugs the lads, drunkenly*). LADS I LOVE YE!

(*Might start singing the song/chant from earlier again, or 'Olé, olé, olé' etc.*)

DYLAN (*calls*). You gonna come with us, Emma?

Be a shame for only Paul to see that nice ass.

PAUL. I don't know if it's Emma's scene.

EMMA *emerges in her underwear. Grabs something to cover herself.*

EMMA. What's my scene?

SEAN. Will the missus be there, Paul, what?

DYLAN. Turn around there.

She doesn't turn.

DYLAN *takes a sneaky photo.*

SEAN (*drunk and high on testosterone*). Lads lads lads!

EMMA *looks drugged and a bit haggard.*

EMMA (*to* PAUL). Did you not lock the door?

PAUL. Did I not?

SEAN (*drunk*). Mammy O'Donovan wouldn't like this at all.

EMMA. What did you say about my mother?

SEAN. Just said Emma O'Donovan's not like that.

Beat.

EMMA. What am I like then?

DYLAN. Paul'll have to fill us in later. Or you might demonstrate yourself.

Beat. EMMA *looks ashamed and angry, but won't show it.*

Where's Zoe? She not joining us?

EMMA. She's not interested, Dylan.

It's never going to happen.

DYLAN. Alright, princess. Did *I say I* was interested? Stuck-up –

PAUL (*with the drugs*). So you gonna join us, darling?

Pause.

DYLAN *cackles.*

DYLAN. Emma O'Donovan wouldn't take pills. Not even prescription ones. You wouldn't pollute that perfect body, would you? Those perfect tits and that glorious ass.

Semi-mocking, DYLAN *gets down to worship her body.*

The boys laugh.

DYLAN *gets up.*

(*Change of tone.*) Nah, O'Donovan's too good for us.

EMMA *laughs, darkly.*

She takes one.

EMMA (*stares at* DYLAN). Don't tell me what I am.

(*To the room, angry bravado.*) Did someone say something about another party?

SEAN and PAUL cheer. DYLAN looks at her with appetite.

Her towel or cover may drop or she may trip. The boys laugh.

DYLAN picks up the towel and as she lunges for it, he moves it again, she trips slightly again.

They move in around her. She looks like she's getting limper and more unresponsive. SEAN might take out his phone and drunkenly try to take a selfie with them in the background.

He might pause at the edge as if he might be sick.

Drugged-up music, dance, blurring, tension building.

Lights darken.

EMMA sends five blank texts to ZOE. The messages start to flood the screen, in flashes like photos.

BLACKOUT. Hold the blackout. Maybe some more flashes after the blackout, and a sense of spreading, the images spreading.

Slowly her parents light up.

Parents look as if they have just found her on the front porch. They don't move as they speak to each other.

MAM. Help me. Help me, Denis, for God's sake. We need to get her inside.

Emma, get up.

She's burning up. Look at those blisters. She's burning up.

Feel her forehead, Denis. Denis, would you stop standing there like an idiot and help me.

Pick her up, for God's sake, would you move.

BRYAN appears.

BRYAN. What the – ?

Why are you back early?

MAM. It's 4 p.m. in the afternoon, Bryan. You had *one job*.

BRYAN. She's eighteen. She's just drunk.

He sort-of laughs.

MAM. We arrive home to find her dumped like a piece of rubbish outside the door, lying unconscious on the porch for everyone to see. This is funny?

BRYAN.…No.

MAM. I thought she was *dead*.

Cover her up as you carry her, Denis. Dear God, is she not wearing any –

Mind the rug.

Lights come up to see EMMA *onstage alone. She lies strewn like rubbish on the ground.*

EMMA *gets sick on the rug.*

Lights down on family.

EMMA *tries to put on her school uniform.*

She hears these voices, both boys and girls.

SPEECH. Have you seen the photos?

Go on Facebook.

Check Snapchat.

It's like porn.

It's outrageous.

Liar.

Lads, lads, lads, big night.

Fuck, my head.

Still sore.

What a sesh.

Easy Emma Facebook page.

Skank.

But, was she even awake?

She was high.

She's a bitch, though.

She's a whore, I heard.

I'd say she was asking for it.

She steps out, as she did in Scene One. Her friends light up.

ALI. Sorry, that seat is taken.

MAGGIE. You seemed pretty friendly with Eli on Saturday night.

ZOE. Friendly with a lot of people.

ALI. Like Paul wasn't enough you had to ride Sean too and fucking Dylan Walsh. What is wrong with you? You're actually sick, Emma, *you're sick.*

You knew what I felt about Sean, but it didn't matter. Whatever Emma O'Donovan wants, Emma O'Donovan gets, right? You've never been a good friend, ever, and none of us have ever said anything about it, but this is… this is…

EMMA *puts her head down between her knees for a minute as if for breath.*

MAGGIE. Are you okay, Emma?

EMMA *can't speak. She tries, but nothing comes out. She shakes her head.*

Pause.

ZOE. That's right. Best not to say anything.

No one likes a girl who makes a fuss.

Beat. ZOE *sees that* EMMA *looks genuinely bewildered.*

You sent me five blank texts on Saturday night. What were you trying to say?

No response. EMMA *can't remember anything.*

You might want to check your Facebook.

Lights down on everyone.

EMMA *alone*.

EMMA. I check my Facebook.

Pale limbs, long hair, head lolling back on to the pillow. The photos start at the head, work down the body, lingering on the naked flesh spread across the rose-covered sheets.

Me.

Dylan on top of that girl. His hands over her face as if to cover it up.

Me.

In the next photos his fingers are inside the girl, but she doesn't move. He gives the camera a thumbs-up. They all laugh as

Her head and shoulders have fallen off the edge of the bed, he spreads her legs, the next photos are pink flesh. Screenshots of Snapchats of pink flesh.

That's me. I am pink flesh.

Who's taking the photos?

Then Paul holds her legs up in the air. Dylan puts his face between her legs and grimaces like it smells.

Now it's Sean. No. Sean who gave me a Valentine's card once. He trips, he falls, he has a bleary-eyed smile on his face. He is so drunk.

He climbs on the bed. He gets on top of the girl. More photos. He vomits on her hair. His sister goes out with my brother. He vomits on my hair.

Then she's on the ground. She lies there. Photo after photo, how many people have seen this? Dylan stands above her, his dick in his hand and a thin yellow stream flowing from him on to her head.

Someone comments, 'Some people deserve to be pissed on.'

Some people deserve it. It gets a hundred and eighty-eight likes.

End of Act.

ACT TWO

Scene One

CONOR *has come to visit* EMMA *at home.*

He brings flowers.

CONOR. Your mam let me in. Looks sore.

EMMA. It'll go away.

CONOR. Has to get worse to get better.

Do you have Aloe Vera?

EMMA. Yeah. No. Chamomile lotion.

CONOR. I got sunburnt once. In Spain.

EMMA. Yeah?

CONOR. Sorry, I don't know what else to say.

EMMA. Okay.

CONOR. No, I mean about anything.

EMMA. Yeah.

It's not that big a deal.

CONOR. I wanted to come yesterday. I wanted to come as soon as I saw the Facebook page.

EMMA. You've seen the page?

Beat.

It's okay.

Sorry.

CONOR. Don't apologise.

Beat.

EMMA. I suppose everyone has seen it. Absolutely everyone has seen it at this stage.

CONOR *doesn't answer.*

CONOR. Do you want me to bring over Aloe Vera?

EMMA. No.

Beat.

CONOR. It's good that the guards are involved now.

I hope they –

EMMA. Who told you that?

CONOR. Sorry?

EMMA. How do you know that?

CONOR. Oh. Uh. Sean called me.

But I told him I never want to speak to him –

EMMA. How did Sean know?

CONOR. Dr Casey is friends with Sergeant Sutton.

But, Emma, I told him I never want to speak to him again.

EMMA (*misplaced anger*). Don't be ridiculous, Conor, Sean didn't even do that much, he was just... drunk.

CONOR (*misplaced anger*). I saw the fucking photos, Emma, I know what they did to you.

Pause.

EMMA *is upset.*

Sorry. I didn't mean to shout. I'm just.

It's okay. Emmie, it's okay. I'm here.

He goes to comfort her.

It'll all be okay. It's okay.

It's okay. Don't cry.

I'll take care of you.

I'm here now.

Beat. She relaxes into him. He rubs her shoulder.

EMMA. Your neck is red.

CONOR. Is it?

EMMA. You always get that when you're nervous.

Remember we cut the hair off the Barbies in your house and then we said it wasn't us. You had a red neck then.

CONOR. Did I?

EMMA. You did.

I remember thinking you couldn't tell a lie without your body betraying you.

EMMA *starts to touch his neck.*

I remember thinking you were such a good person.

CONOR *looks uncomfortable.*

Too good for me.

So good I didn't know why you wanted me.

CONOR (*trying to keep it light*). Don't. It's ticklish.

EMMA *touches his thigh instead.*

EMMA. Is that better?

CONOR *moves his leg slightly away.*

Do you like that?

She keeps rubbing it higher and higher. He pulls it away.

CONOR. Emmie.

EMMA. What? Sssh.

She leans in to kiss him. She does small kisses from his neck to his mouth. He lets her kiss him for a moment on the mouth even though he isn't responding.

He then pulls away and stands up.

Beat.

What's wrong?

CONOR. I. Just.

EMMA. Isn't this what you've always wanted?

CONOR. Yeah, but.

EMMA. But what?

CONOR. Not… like this, Em.

EMMA. Why not?

Are you afraid someone will come in?

I can lock the door.

CONOR *shakes his head*.

Then what?

CONOR. I don't want you to…

EMMA. Yeah?

CONOR. Feel like you have to do this.

EMMA. I don't 'have to' do this. I want to do this.

CONOR. I just.

EMMA (*mockery*). 'I just.'

CONOR. Emma.

He looks at her. She interprets it as pity.

Pause.

EMMA. I'm no good to you any more.

Your future wifey is tainted.

CONOR. That's not fair.

EMMA. Why did you come?

CONOR. Sorry?

EMMA. Why are you here?

CONOR. …To see how you were.

EMMA. To assess the damage.

Beat.

I'd like to be alone now.

CONOR. Emmie.

EMMA. Please go home.

CONOR. Em, c'mon.

EMMA. C'mon what? I belong to everyone now.

I want to be alone.

Get out of my room.

Pause. They look at each other. She turns away. He looks like he might cry. He waits a moment, turns and then leaves.

I am *That Girl*. And I can't stop this. There's no way I can stop this now.

She puts the flowers in the bin.

THIS YEAR

Scene Two

A year later.

Radio voices, play to an empty room.

MAN 1. It's as simple as this, Ned.

I'm not a judgmental man. But if this girl was in the bed with the lad anyway, what was she expecting?

PRESENTER. I don't think she was expecting to get raped, Davey. Although yours does seem to be a popular opinion. You agree with him, do you, Eileen?

WOMAN. I do. I see these girls walking around here on a Saturday night, half-naked –

MAN 1. They are –

WOMAN. Skirts up to their backside and tops down to their belly buttons. And they're drinking too much and falling over in the streets, they're practically advertising to be attacked. As that other man says, what do they expect?

PRESENTER (*unsure*). Right, well there's some would say we should turn the focus on to the young men involved.

At some point during the above, DAD enters and turns off the radio. He then exits for work.

Beat.

He returns, checks the sole of his shoe, puts down his case, gets a dustpan and goes back out.

MAM *comes in and turns the radio back on.*

The following is heard.

We have to take a break now, and it's time for the news, but stay with us as we'll keep discussing the Ballinatoom case. It's one year on this weekend from that disturbing case in County Cork where an eighteen-year-old schoolgirl known as the Ballinatoom Girl…

At some point during the above DAD enters.

DAD. Turn that off.

MAM. What's –

DAD. The radio. Turn it off. There's shit on the step (now).

MAM. What?

DAD stands with a bag of poo in his hand.

Well, don't just stand there, Denis. Get rid of it.

DAD. Where will I put it?

MAM. In the brown bin, or somewhere.

DAD. Jesus.

Beat.

MAM. Watch your good suit.

DAD. I'm not going to leave a turd on the front doorstep, am I? I nearly stood in it.

Do I have anything on my shoe?

He lifts one leg. MAM *looks.*

MAM. No.

Why your best suit?

DAD....meetings today.

MAM. Important?

DAD. Maybe.

MAM. Ciaran O'Brien, is it?

DAD *goes outside to dispose of the turd.*

Anything in particular, or do you know?

He comes back in and washes his hands.

DAD. What? No nothing. Right.

MAM (*about her baking*). If you wait a minute, you can take one of these with you.

DAD. I'll be late.

MAM (*coaching him, fixing his tie or something*). What difference will a minute make, love. Breathe.

Beat.

What do you think that's all about anyhow?

DAD. I don't know what he wants, I said I don't know.

MAM. No the... the doorstep.

Beat.

Just kids, probably.

DAD. Yeah.

MAM. Nothing better to be doing.

DAD. Mmm.

Pause. DAD *stews.*

Unless it's some reaction.

MAM. Reaction to what?

DAD. To the news.

Beat.

MAM. But we only just got that news.

DAD. Yeah.

MAM. I mean we've really just heard about that.

DAD. Yeah, I know.

I don't know.

MAM. Who would react like that, anyhow? Only an animal.

DAD. There's a lot of people won't be happy.

Lots of people will be angry at this... development.

MAM. Should we call the guards?

DAD. About what?

MAM. This morning.

DAD. Nora.

MAM. What?

DAD. A turd?

MAM. Well I don't know. Intimidation.

DAD. Call Sutton about a bag of dogshit on the doorstep? Haven't they heard enough, too much, from us? No, we won't call the guards.

Beat.

And it was probably kids. Meaningless. That's what you said.

MAM. She does have a lot of support, too, you know.

Even last month at the Farmers' Market, there were quite a few people sympathising at the stall.

DAD. You make it sound as if she's –

MAM. You know what I mean

There's lots of support for Emma. This is good news we've got.

DAD. It is.

Sees the prospectuses.

What are these?

MAM. Prospectuses. Books for college courses.

DAD. I know what a prospectus is.

MAM. Ms McCarthy dropped them in.

DAD. And when was she here?

MAM. Yesterday. Or, maybe the day before.

DAD. Did you tell her the news?

MAM. I don't remember.

DAD. When was she here?

MAM. It might have been the day before.

DAD. We'd want to keep track of who we're talking to.

Beat.

MAM. Ms McCarthy isn't leaving excrement on our doorstep, Denis.

And I doubt she was telling her students to go out and do that either.

DAD. I didn't mean… ha.

MAM. It was she that called attention to all this.

DAD. It was.

MAM. …called the guards in the first place… We should be grateful to Ms McCarthy.

Beat.

DAD. And did Emma look at any prospectus?

MAM. I'm sure she has.

EMMA!

EMMA *appears. Not in uniform.*

DAD. She's not in uniform.

EMMA. No.

Looks to MAM *and then to* DAD.

Should I be?

MAM (*weak performance for* DAD)....it's a school day. You should be going to school.

EMMA (*to* DAD). Are you not going to work today?

DAD. I got delayed.

DAD *goes to exit.*

He's about to leave without kissing MAM, *as was always their habit.*

MAM. Say goodbye.

She goes to him and kisses him. It's a little awkward.

He leaves.

EMMA. There's a... smell.

Looks around.

Someone has dog poo on their shoe.

MAM. You must look at those books Ms McCarthy brought round, Em.

EMMA. I will.

(*To audience.*) I promise to look at them. I take them to my room, and throw them in the bin. The next morning the bin will be emptied, no mention of the discarded brochures. And on it goes, my world gets smaller and smaller, wrapping itself around me.

MAM. What do you think about school, so?

EMMA. I'm not feeling well today.

MAM. No?

EMMA. I couldn't sleep last night.

Beat. They feel the weight of the anniversary weekend.

MAM. Even with the tablets?

EMMA. I was having bad dreams.

Beat.

MAM. That's strange with the tablets.

EMMA. Yeah. Maybe I need to increase my dose.

Beat.

MAM. You can come to the stall with me. You need to leave the house.

EMMA. What time is Bryan coming?

MAM. Later.

EMMA. What time?

MAM. I can't answer that.

EMMA. The milk is off again.

MAM. Is it?

EMMA. It's all clumpy and smells like sour cream.

MAM. I'll buy more. Don't tell Dad.

EMMA. Is something burning?

MAM (*outburst*). Jesus Christ, the fucking muffins. They'll be ruined!

For God's sake, arriving with burnt goods on top of everything else.

EMMA *looks on.*

Get out of the way, would you!

Elsewhere.

A digital element accompanies the following speech, tweets and news items fill the screen.

EMMA. The journey back from the market is quiet, my mother clearly not daring to turn on the radio this weekend. My therapist insists I keep a diary. I make a list.

Reasons why people are still interested in the Ballinatoom Case one year on:

Three boys, one girl.

The effect of social media on young people today.

When will young people learn the value of privacy?

Does 'jock culture' support rape culture?

Does 'rape culture' even exist?

One in three reported rapes happen when the victim has been drinking.

We need to talk about consent.

Three middle-class boys' futures lie in jeopardy.

Maybe I was asking for it.

Scene Three

BRYAN *has arrived.*

BRYAN. Oh, and hey look at this, this guy is one of the first fish to come out of the sea and live on land. Here, let me get it up.

Look at it.

He takes out his phone.

It's called a tiktaalik.

EMMA. Tiktaalik?

It's gross-looking. Ugh.

BRYAN. Yeah.

Fish like tiktaalik gave rise to, like, reptiles and mammals.

EMMA. Are we descended from fish now? I thought it was apes.

BRYAN. What do you think?

He holds up the phone to his face as if to compare himself to the fish.

EMMA. Uncanny.

BRYAN *laughs*.

BRYAN. Sense of humour's on the return, is it?

I missed this girl.

EMMA (*to audience*). It's only Bryan, I have to tell myself as he feels me stiffen.

Bryan won't hurt me.

He gives her a hug. She stiffens a bit.

BRYAN. Oh sorry. I didn't think.

Beat.

Anyhow, Em. This is great news.

EMMA. Yeah.

She yawns.

BRYAN. Tired?

EMMA. A bit.

BRYAN. It's draining.

EMMA. Yeah.

BRYAN. But, as fucking annoying as the relentless radio and TV is, it means people are thinking about… this stuff, they're interested.

EMMA. Yeah.

BRYAN. No?

EMMA. Yeah, it means they love the drama of it.

Beat.

BRYAN. Well, you could be surprised.

MAM *enters, carrying the bottle of champagne* BRYAN *brought.*

MAM *looking at label.*

MAM. Imagine. Non-alcoholic.

BRYAN. Still, the same idea.

MAM. Yeah, no, that's great.

BRYAN. It's just for some…

MAM. Fizz.

BRYAN. Yeah. We could have it tonight.

MAM. Or for breakfast.

BRYAN. Yeah.

MAM. With orange juice.

EMMA. A *mimosa.*

MAM. Yeah, a mimosa. That's what they call it.

They do them at the market now, too.

BRYAN. It's a celebration. Em?

EMMA. Sure.

BRYAN. It is. This is the best news we've had all year. The DPP doesn't take on every case.

We should mark the occasion.

MAM. Absolutely. Thank you, Bryan.

BRYAN. For Emma.

MAM. Yes.

Yes, absolutely.

Beat.

A glass of real wine, Bryan, while we wait for Dad?

BRYAN. No, thanks.

MAM. Emma doesn't mind. Do you, Emma?

EMMA. No. I don't mind.

BRYAN. Actually, I'm not drinking myself. For the time being, anyhow.

Beat.

MAM. Okay.

BRYAN. The lady I'm seeing at UL, the therapist there, she said –

MAM (*shutting down*). Oh, right.

BRYAN *looks like he's about to say more, then decides against it. He rolls his eyes.*

BRYAN. She says a lot of interesting things actually…

EMMA (*to audience*). Therapy equals depression equals things we don't talk about in this family.

MAM. Have a muffin.

BRYAN. Maybe later.

MAM. I made a lot.

EMMA. They didn't sell.

MAM. It's not to do with… anything. I made too many, that's all. And the rain would keep people away. Terrible rain.

EMMA (*to audience*). Pink flesh. Legs spread. They have seen the photos too.

Beat.

BRYAN. Yeah, there was a bad crash on the road on the way down.

MAM. Was there?

BRYAN. Looked like there might have been a child involved.

MAM. That's terrible.

You'd think with the roads improving... Still, slippy. Terrible rain.

BRYAN. Speed, I suppose.

Beat.

MAM. That's it.

Beat.

BRYAN. How was school this week, Emmie? What did *you* learn?

EMMA....Nothing much.

BRYAN. Did you go to school today?

Beat.

MAM. She had therapy today.

BRYAN. During the day? Who arranged that?

Beat.

What about yesterday?

EMMA. We went to see Aidan then. To confirm the news.

BRYAN. Did you go to school at all this week?

Beat.

(*To* MAM.) Why didn't Emma go to school?

MAM. She was tired, Bryan. Look at her.

BRYAN. Emma has to go to school.

He's about to say more.

DAD *enters.*

DAD (*a performance*). There he is! The big man himself. Did you bring the weather from Limerick?

You're welcome home.

BRYAN. Thanks, Dad.

DAD. You brought your laundry with you, I see.

BRYAN. I did.

DAD. Good man. Your mother'll do that for you.

BRYAN. Ah... cheers.

I was just saying to Mam –

MAM. Oh yes.

DAD. What's that now?

MAM. There was a terrible accident on the road coming down, could have been a child injured.

Beat.

DAD. Was there? I didn't hear that.

BRYAN. Yeah.

DAD. The rain I suppose. And imagine this time last year it was...

Beat.

EMMA (*to audience*). This time last year it was sunny. This time last year we were in the middle of a heatwave, waiting for it to break. This time last year, we were normal.

BRYAN. I was also saying –

MAM (*to* DAD). You're delayed.

DAD. Went through Kilgavan on the way home.

MAM. Why?

DAD. For petrol. It's a nice spin.

How do you reckon it'll go tonight, Bryan?

BRYAN. Hah?

DAD. The game.

BRYAN. Oh, right. I don't know.

DAD. C'mon now. Who'll take it?

BRYAN. Haven't really been following, Dad, to be honest.

DAD. Could have been you on the pitch one time.

BRYAN (*dismissive, but lightly*). Ah, now. Not so much.

DAD. You playing any football at all these days?

> BRYAN *shakes his head*.

> You'll have to get back to it.

> Well, we'll watch it together this evening. Yeah?

BRYAN. I guess.

DAD. Put a nice fire on, put the feet up…

BRYAN. Yeah, unless Emma would like to watch something else together.

DAD.…a few beers. Hah?

BRYAN. I dunno… Like a movie. *Michael Collins* is on.

EMMA. No. I'm fine. I don't really want to see *Michael Collins*.

BRYAN. Or, you could watch the match with us.

> *Beat*.

DAD (*not looking at her*). Emma doesn't like sport. Do you, Emma?

EMMA. Not really.

DAD. See?

> DAD *is starting to get annoyed now*.

> *Beat*.

MAM. Bryan brought champagne.

DAD. For what?

MAM. To celebrate the news.

DAD. I thought we might have a night off from the news.

MAM. It was thoughtful, Denis, to bring… well, fake champagne.

BRYAN. It's not fake. Just non-alcoholic.

Awkward pause. MAM *puts cutlery on the table.*

What did Aidan say this week? He said it was good news, didn't he?

MAM. Yes, he did.

BRYAN. Even though they're still pleading 'not guilty'. I don't know what judge or jury would look at those photos and see anything other than guilty.

Beat.

EMMA. They might not be able to use the photos, Aidan said.

BRYAN. What?

Beat.

MAM. Yes that's right, I was going to tell you. We just heard that.

BRYAN. But, the photos are the whole case.

EMMA (*to audience*). Does Bryan think of those photos when he looks at me now?

DAD. There must be other stuff in the book of evidence. They're not sure about the... It's all unchartered territory. Facebook, Snapchat...

BRYAN. They have to use the fucking photos.

DAD. I'll call Aidan on Monday and he'll tell me.

MAM. He can't tell you.

DAD. I'll call him.

BRYAN (*not directed at anyone, he might bang something*). Fuck's sake. Fuck this.

Call him now, so. You might still catch him.

MAM. He can't tell him, he hasn't access / to the book of evidence.

BRYAN. We need an answer, Dad, do it before he's gone.

DAD. I'll call him Monday, I said.

BRYAN. For God's sake, we'll have it hanging over us all weekend then.

DAD. I've had a very long day. Let's keep it civil this evening.

BRYAN. You haven't said a word to Emma since you got in, Dad.

DAD. Have I not?

BRYAN. No.

DAD. You're not home for weeks, so park it please with the commentary, alright?

Pause.

MAM. Come on now. This is nice. The four of us all here together for the weekend.

Beat.

BRYAN. I'm going to empty my bag.

Beat.

He leaves.

Pause.

EMMA. Can I have my tablet now?

MAM. This early?

EMMA. I'm tired. I want to go to sleep.

MAM looks at DAD. *He shrugs.*

MAM. Okay.

She counts the tablets routinely and then gives EMMA *her tablet.*

Show me.

EMMA *sticks out her tongue.*

Goodnight, love.

EMMA. Night.

As she's almost gone, MAM *looks at* DAD. DAD *reluctantly, and not looking at* EMMA, *actively looking away, speaks.*

DAD. Night.

EMMA *leaves.*

MAM. Kilgavan?

DAD. That Dylan Walsh lad is working down the road now. At the garage.

MAM. Right.

DAD. He's dropped out of school it seems. Another fallout.

MAM. I suppose.

DAD. And Sean Casey has lost his shot at the county, I hear.

MAM. Well.

DAD. Well. Did you think I was off with some other woman, did you?

MAM. No.

Were you?

DAD. I was driving half an hour out of town to get five cent more expensive petrol.

Beat.

Ciaran O'Brien is moving his account now too. On account of Paul. On account of all this. Conflict of interest. Et cetera.

Beat.

MAM. Good riddance, Denis. I don't know how you were still meeting with that man anyhow.

DAD. Business doesn't work like that, Nora.

MAM. No. Well.

DAD. He's the bank's biggest customer. If he goes, they'll all start –

Pause. DAD *shakes it off, and puts on a braver face.*

How did you get on at the market today, anyhow?

Beat.

MAM. Despite the rain, terrific. A good day, by any standard.

Scene Four

EMMA. I wake in the middle of the night. I remember. I am pink flesh. I am splayed legs. All the photos and photos and photos.

I cannot remember, so those photos and comments have become my memories.

I flick through the local newspaper until I find what I am looking for. I am back in the newspapers this weekend.

EMMA *reads from a newspaper.*

EMMA *looks up.*

'The Ballinatoom Girl should ask a few questions of herself.'

I read about the Ballinatoom Girl as if she's not me. Sometimes I almost wonder who she is, why she was so stupid, and then I remember.

BRYAN *enters. She pushes the paper aside.*

BRYAN. Emma?

EMMA. What are you doing?

BRYAN. Sitting here in the dark.

EMMA. I like it like that.

He switches on a main light.

That hurts.

BRYAN. Give over.

EMMA. Why are you up?

BRYAN (*goes to get a glass of milk*). I… just need a drink.

Why are *you* up?

EMMA. I was awake.

BRYAN. What are you reading?

EMMA. Nothing. Local… stuff.

Could you not sleep?

BRYAN. What about?

Beat.

EMMA. Community spirit.

Beat.

BRYAN. Hmmmm.

He looks at her for more.

EMMA. And the Celtic Tiger. How it ruined young people. Especially girls.

BRYAN. What's the link, exactly?

EMMA. I don't know. Too many short skirts.

BRYAN. Huh. Want some?

EMMA *shakes her head.*

EMMA. And how the Ballinatoom Girl should think of the community whose foundations she is tearing apart at the seams.

Pause.

BRYAN *grabs the paper off her.*

BRYAN (*chastising*). Emma.

EMMA. Do you ever talk to Jen?

BRYAN *gives her a look.*

BRYAN. No.

EMMA. What?

BRYAN. Why?

EMMA. Maybe you should get in touch with her –

BRYAN. Not at the moment.

EMMA. I wouldn't mind. I –

BRYAN. I know. If I wanted to, I would.

EMMA. None of this is anything to do with her.

Beat.

She's obviously going to stand by Sean if that's what it is, / they're family…

BRYAN. And that's that then. I'm sure she's fine.

EMMA. But you were so good for –

BRYAN. Things change.

EMMA. Yeah, but don't you miss her?

BRYAN. Don't you worry about it.

EMMA. And you don't know how she might be feeling / either –

BRYAN. I'm a grown man, thanks, I can advocate for myself.

EMMA. You have terrible bags under your eyes, Bryan. And you're thin. And it's making me feel –

BRYAN. I'm studying a lot.

Beat.

And you should be too.

EMMA *gets up to leave.* BRYAN *softens, changes tack.*

Let's do something tomorrow.

EMMA. No.

(*To audience.*) No, no, no, the word rolls off my tongue so easily now.

(*To* BRYAN.) No thanks.

BRYAN. Do you have any other plans for tomorrow?

EMMA. Um. I'm not sure yet... Maybe.

BRYAN. Come on, Em. I'm trying.

EMMA (*to audience*). But I don't want him to try. I don't want him to have to try all the time.

BRYAN. Emma?

EMMA (*to audience*). He needs me to say that I'm okay. He needs to know that I won't do anything stupid.

(*To* BRYAN.) The last time we went out everyone stared at me.

BRYAN. Everyone has always stared at you.

EMMA (*to audience*). I encouraged it. I wanted them to stare. I liked it then.

(*To* BRYAN.) I don't like it any more.

Beat.

BRYAN. Fine, don't bother your arse to do anything.

BRYAN *leaves*.

EMMA. I make another list.

I count the things he could do if it wasn't for me.

Hang out with Jen.

Remember what a genuine smile feels like.

Have a good time.

Be normal.

He could be happy. They could all be happy.

EMMA *leaves*.

Lights come up.

It is morning. DAD *enters, he sees the paper on the table face-down. He picks it up and goes to put it in the recycling hurriedly as* MAM *comes in, holding a bottle of wine.*

DAD *jumps*.

MAM. You're as bad as Emma.

DAD. You gave me a fright.

I thought I had this binned.

He still has the paper in his hand.

MAM. I didn't touch it.

DAD. Wine?

MAM (*the bottle*). I'm putting it away.

It was left out.

DAD *looks suspicious*.

Beat.

DAD. Did you read this?

MAM. I had a look.

DAD. And the other article at the front, did you see that one?

MAM. Yes.

DAD. Are some of her friends talking to the papers, do you think?

'A source in the local Garda station says that the alleged victim was well known locally for her promiscuous behavior.'

MAM. Says who? What source?

DAD. Does she *have* any friends?

MAM. Of course she does, Denis.

Pause.

DAD. And how long did it take for any of them to come forward? You know? That's what really gets me. Why did it take so long for any of them to come forward?

The boys have character testimonies coming out their eyeballs from the beginning.

You have to ask, Nora, when you read stuff like this, do we know her at all?

MAM. Keep your voice down unless you want another trip to A and E this weekend.

Beat.

DAD. It's just a question. We're going to have to get used to difficult questions.

Beat.

(*Waving the newspaper.*) You know what this means?

MAM. What?

DAD. It means there'll be a counter-case, or an accusation, about... her history now.

MAM. History?

DAD. ...sexual... history... She'll have to testify now, she'll need legal representation too.

MAM. We don't know that yet.

DAD. If they can prove, or insinuate, she was... promiscuous, which it looks like they can...

MAM. We brought Emmie up well. She's not like that.

DAD. Oh come off it, Nora.

MAM. It's one article.

DAD. It's all the papers.

MAM. They're trying to *sell* papers, they don't *know* what happened. They don't know *her*.

And what does that mean anyhow? Does the fact that, that lads were often after her make her 'promiscuous' now? She's a pretty girl, she always has been, is that Emma's fault?

There's comments online about her being on that billboard after the football gala that time as if, as if it's evidence against her, and who put her up there? They all did.

DAD. How did you not know what she was up to?

MAM. Me?

DAD. You're her mother. Did you not have some kind of *talk* with her –

MAM. And you have no role to play?

Beat.

DAD. I'm just out there every day listening to this.

The things being said... the details they discuss... And it's not discreet, Nora, they *want* me to hear it. And I just have to stand there?

And sometimes, you know, I know she's our daughter, but sometimes you have to wonder...

MAM *starts to cry.*

Don't cry, Nora. I can't.

Don't.

Beat.

He goes to leave.

MAM. Where are you going?

DAD. I need some air.

He leaves.

MAM *pours herself another glass of wine.*

BRYAN *enters.*

BRYAN. Where's Dad gone?

MAM. He had to go out.

BRYAN. It's not even twelve.

MAM. He's a lot on. I'm sorry, darling.

I'm sorry we're not a normal family right now.

BRYAN. What does that mean?

MAM. Hopefully we go back soon. When this is… (over.)

Beat.

You've always been such a wonderful son.

She tries to hug him. She's a bit drunk.

Are the women chasing you in Limerick?

BRYAN. I don't notice if they are. Have you been drinking?

MAM. You're not still upset about Jen?

Silence.

BRYAN. Don't let Emma on her laptop or phone today.

.   Okay?

Do you hear me?

MAM (*not listening*). Yes, darling.

BRYAN. Now that that crap is out.

MAM. I remember so well giving birth to my beautiful son.
And you were so big and strong and gorgeous, and so
pleasant; such a lovely smile. And then a daughter. And I had
the perfect family. A 'gentleman's family'. And so handsome
both of you. Everyone always said to me 'you have the most
beautiful family'.

BRYAN (*picks up the paper*). Why is this still knocking about?

BRYAN *is now reading the paper.*

MAM. When I had my little cancer scare last year, Bryan, my
first thought was how sad I would be… up there, or
wherever, without my lovely family, and not to see either of
you get married or have your own children.

BRYAN *is shocked at the paper.*

BRYAN. Veronica fucking Horan.

He looks at MAM.

MAM. What?

BRYAN. Jen's mam is probably back in John of Gods by the sounds of this.

Beat.

Hah?

'The mother of one of the accused, vulnerable after the death of a son many years ago, is reported to be suffering from a nervous breakdown… Has the Ballinatoom Girl given any thought to this poor woman and her emotional well-being?'

MAM. I thought you would have heard from one of your friends.

BRYAN. Well I didn't.

MAM (*as in 'so what?'*). And?

BRYAN. Jen'll be fucking devastated by this. You know we worried about her mam.

MAM. Jen's mam. Boohoo Jen's mam. Wouldn't I love the luxury of a nervous breakdown. And it's pathetic using John Junior as some kind of excuse; it's over ten years ago now.

EMMA *enters.*

BRYAN (*to* EMMA). Did you know about this?

MAM. Don't show Emma that.

EMMA. I've already read it.

BRYAN. Why didn't you tell me about Anne Casey?

EMMA. I tried to bring it up last night. I told you I felt bad / about Jen –

MAM. What does it matter, Bryan? She's not talking to you, is she? She doesn't want anything to do with this family, and we don't want anything to do with hers.

BRYAN *starts to leave.*

So grow up, Bryan! Get real.

He's gone.

What are you looking at?

I was defending you, wasn't I?

Beat.

EMMA (*to audience*). I am a small child and I lose sight of my mother at a crowded shopping centre. I look up at the lady next to me, putting my hand around her knees, but then I see it isn't Mam and panic begins to pool in my throat. The seconds slow down, everyone walking past me as if they are wading through water, and I believe, in that moment, that I will never find my mother, that I will never see her again.

MAM. Is this what your brother should be coming home to?

EMMA. Can I have my phone today?

MAM *looks at her.*

MAM *shrugs.*

MAM. Whatever you like.

Images of drowning flood the screen.

Scene Five

BRYAN *starts an email to Jen.*

BRYAN. Dear Jen. Jen, I know you don't want to talk to me – but I read the article in the paper, and I was sorry to hear about your mom. I'm sorry I didn't hear sooner. I think everyone assumed I would have heard.

I wish I could comfort you through this, and vice versa, and it's so fucked up the positions we're in. I still think of you all the time. Being back in Ballinatoom is fucking hard as I see your face and think of us absolutely everywhere. Ugh, I guess I just really miss you, et cetera. Bryan.

Beat.

EMMA. Send.

BRYAN *sits looking at the screen.*

EMMA *looks at her phone, she sees the new development amongst her peers: images of support for the boys. She looks through several pictures of girls wearing custom-made T-shirts that say #TeamPaul, #TeamDylan, #TeamSean. She is surprised, she looks at more, and more. Images blur before her.*

BRYAN *too, slowly, begins to scroll through his Facebook feed. Images of #TeamPaul, #TeamDylan, #TeamSean. Then he comes to a picture of Jen holding up the T-shirt. He zooms in. He zooms out. BRYAN steps away from the computer. It is overwhelming.*

BRYAN. Fuck it. Look at her.

What am I doing?

BRYAN *paces, retreats from laptop.*

BRYAN *wipes his face in his T-shirt. He pulls it off and puts on a fresh one. The images grow darker, and uglier, in content.*

Elsewhere.

EMMA. I go for new channels. I watch videos filed under Reluctance and Non-consent. They don't use that word either. I watch for clues. Is that what happened to me? Is that what I looked like? Pink flesh, splayed legs. I want to see these girls cry too. I can do this for hours and hours. The videos are something to hold on to, something to ground me, to make sure I don't float away.

BRYAN *enters, he looks at* EMMA *and then the laptop.*

BRYAN (*determined*). You're not allowed that.

She jumps on the bed and knocks the laptop closed. Beat.

EMMA. Mam gave it to me.

He puts his hand out.

BRYAN. Can I have?

EMMA. No.

BRYAN. Why not?

EMMA. I need it.

BRYAN. For what?

EMMA.... A project.

BRYAN. What project?

EMMA. It helps my brain switch off.

BRYAN. So does exercise.

EMMA. Mam understands that.

BRYAN. Go for a walk.

EMMA. I don't want to go outside.

BRYAN. You're not supposed to have it, are you?

EMMA. What's *wrong* with you?

BRYAN. I don't care what Mam understands, or clearly doesn't.
Now give it.

He puts his hand out again.

Beat.

Come on.

She hands it over.

I'm sorry.

Elsewhere.

Doors slam.

DAD. What would you like me to do? A course of *action* please
here, Nora.

MAM. I'd like you to be a fucking man, for once.

DAD. What does that mean?

MAM. She's your daughter too.

DAD. What does that mean *to be a man*?

MAM *pulls off her coat and scarf. Dumps her bag. They try to keep their voices down.*

I made a decision earlier to –

MAM. You left me on my own.

DAD. It could have been a protest. Did you think of that?

MAM. It wasn't, Denis. It was lying down like a dead dog.

DAD (*defensive*). I'm sorry that you saw it like that, but you didn't have to –

MAM *opens the fridge door and closes it again.*

Back to EMMA.

EMMA. Sorry, sorry, sorry, sorry, everyone is sorry, we're all so sorry.

Elsewhere.

DAD. You didn't have to –

BRYAN *enters on parents.*

They stop and look at him.

BRYAN. Emma's looking up some fucked-up shit online. I looked at her history from last night.

She shouldn't be allowed access to her phone and laptop at all.

I told you that. The therapist told you that.

She can't be looking at this stuff.

She needs her strength up for this trial.

Beat.

MAM. Okay, love. Thanks.

DAD. Any other tips on parenting, Bryan?

Beat.

BRYAN. That's it for now.

Beat.

DAD. Okay then. Off you go.

BRYAN. I'd prefer not to have to give them.

    Beat.

DAD. You'd swear I was the one accused in all this.

    Beat.

    DAD *leaves.*

MAM. Where are you going?

DAD. Out.

MAM. Not again. Jesus, I'm sorry I said anything…

    Come back…

    He's gone.

    Fucking go then.

    MAM *opens the fridge and pours wine.*

BRYAN. Mam.

    The phone rings. Both ignore it at first.

    Mam.

    MAM *answers. No one there.*

    It rings again.

MAM. Leave us alone.

    She hangs up.

    It rings again.

    MAM *drinks.* BRYAN *watches.*

    Back to EMMA.

    She rotates herself around and around in her swivel chair. Her friends, the characters from Act One, from her former world, may appear as a vision as she delivers this speech.

EMMA. Here are the ways I think to end it: fall down stairs, crash car, take too many Xanax, Valium, Venlafaxine, Zopiclone. I ream the drugs off like verbs.

A boy dead on a road. A boy drowned in a slurry pit.

Would my mother rather I was dead? Would that be an easier grief?

I will never have children now. I would not infect them. I would not put them in this world where bad things can happen.

That is a table. That is a chair.

I don't see my friends any more. Maggie was distraught when she found out. Ali wanted to know if it was '*rape* rape', before she 'forgave' me for getting with Sean. I never heard from Zoe. *She's studying so hard*, Maggie said, *she got offered a scholarship dependent on results*. I wish I could tell Zoe I did her a favour. That she is the lucky one.

Conor emails. He says he is looking at photos from when we were children. And that I am beautiful. And that he wants to see me. I don't like when he tells me I'm beautiful. He tells me that Maggie broke up with Eli, because he wouldn't go to the guards. He tells me that Dylan dropped out of school and that he's glad, everyone's glad, that he was always toxic anyhow. He says he went to the open day at Trinity and it looks nice, he thinks Heaney will come up in English and he loves Heaney, didn't I like that poem too? Another poem about a dead boy. No it was Plath I liked, elm tree, and the roots that go into the darkness, and say *do not fear it, I have been there*. I liked that one and the bees, all the bees, and how she tried to reach her father. He tells me, he tells me all the things I'm not around for and I am so grateful. I am so grateful but I can't respond.

Act normal. I tell myself that I must act normal for everyone else. Do it for Bryan. Bryan believes me. Do I believe me?

Draw your body, says the therapist. I draw a squiggle in a corner, *and where are you*, she says?

I point to a dot on the other side of the page.

I am a shadow. I follow around a thing called Emma.

Why were you in the room in the first place, Dad says. *Why were you on the bed?*

Can't we just delete the photos? he said. Can't we just pretend I'm dead.

Visualise a stop sign, I'm told. *When your mind goes into overdrive, visualise a stop sign.*

I want it all to…

EMMA *makes her way downstairs, and pauses outside the living room, hearing her mother singing the first verse of 'Annie's Song'.*

Stop.

Scene Six

MAM *is drinking wine and looking at old photographs. The radio/stereo is playing 'Annie's Song', and she is stopped, singing along to the second verse. She has been crying.*

EMMA *enters.*

MAM *looks up expectantly.*

Beat.

MAM. Oh, it's you.

EMMA…. You're not using a coaster.

MAM *shrugs.*

MAM. What do you want?

EMMA. That's your wedding song.

MAM. It is. And?

Beat.

We had it as our first dance.

EMMA. I know.

MAM. Do you?

EMMA. You used to dance to it with Dad. In the kitchen.

MAM. You noticed that, did you?

EMMA. Of course I did.

It was… nice.

Beat.

I might sleep early. Can I have –

MAM. Look at this one.

MAM *holds out a photo.*

Jimmy Casey.

EMMA….He looks so young.

MAM. Jimmy Casey, how are ya, boy?

He was our best man, did you know that? Sean's uncle, Jimmy Casey.

Beat.

EMMA *nods.*

EMMA. Can I have my tablet?

MAM (*ignoring her*). And look at this one, the great man of the cloth there, look at him, marrying us. The prick.

EMMA. Mam.

MAM. What?

EMMA. I don't know. It's just.

MAM. Are you prudish now?

EMMA. What?

MAM. Is Father Michael not a great man of the cloth?

EMMA. I thought he was your friend.

MAM. No. He's not, it turns out.

Beat.

EMMA. I just want to get my tablet, please.

MAM. Did you not already get it?

EMMA. No.

MAM. Are you stashing extra ones away up there now?

EMMA. No.

MAM. Are we going to find you unconscious again some
morning?

Beat.

Have to keep everything under lock and key around here.

She might get up to get it.

EMMA. You don't *have* to.

MAM stops, turns.

MAM. Did you ever think I'd like to be able to relax in my own
home, Emma?

And not have to see you in a pool of your own blood. The
mess of it everywhere.

EMMA. I'm… sorry.

MAM. No, you're not sorry. You're selfish.

You don't care about me, you don't care about your brother.

EMMA. I do.

MAM. Or your poor father who might be…

EMMA. What?

MAM. Nothing.

EMMA. I'm sorry I made a mess.

MAM. Is that sarcasm?

EMMA. No.

MAM starts to rip out some photos from the album.

MAM. Throw these in the bin, would you?

Who needs these? Lies all of it.

EMMA. Mam, stop it. Stop it, those are our pictures.

She takes the album off MAM.

You're drunk.

MAM. I'm drunk?

EMMA. Aren't you? You're drinking... a lot.

MAM. Am I?

EMMA. Yes, and Dad doesn't like it.

MAM. Does he not?

EMMA. No.

MAM. Is that my fault?

EMMA. You're frightening me, Mam.

MAM. Oh I'm sorry, Emma. I'm sorry to frighten *you*.

Why do you think I'm drunk?

EMMA. I don't know.

MAM. You weren't on Facebook today, no?

EMMA. I'm not allowed on Facebook.

MAM *laughs sarcastically.*

MAM. Since when do you do what you're told?

Beat.

It's all over the internet by now, I'm sure.

EMMA. What is?

MAM. I'm not supposed to say anything, because we're not supposed to upset Emma.

EMMA. I just want to go to bed. Give me the key and I'll get it myself.

MAM *holds out her hand with the key in it, and closes her fist just as* EMMA *reaches for it.*

MAM. Well I think you should know.

Father Michael, the man here who made a speech at my own wedding about loyalty and kindness and friendship. The man who married us, who baptised you two, who buried my poor mother in the ground.

He made a speech at mass today about not judging others, about being 'innocent until proven guilty'. He didn't use any names of course, but everyone knew what he was talking about. You could hear a pin drop in the place.

And me and your father sitting in the front pew like idiots. Like idiots after putting fifty euro in the basket. And your father's neck starts burning up, then, and he won't go up for communion. He won't budge.

Here.

MAM *puts the keys on the table*.

But I went up. I stood up and I walked up there for you, Emma. And my legs were shaking taking it. *Everyone* in the whole church looking at me.

And I passed Ciaran O'Brien on the way down, and do you know what he did?

EMMA. Don't tell me.

MAM. He winked at me.

That's not all of it.

EMMA. Mam, please stop. Don't say anything else, please. I need to go to bed.

EMMA *takes the keys*.

MAM. No, you listen to me, Emma. You stand there and you listen to me like I walked for you today. Father Michael then waits for Paul O'Brien and Sean Casey at the back of the church and he offers condolences and he shakes their hands. In front of the whole congregation.

After all the times we've had that man in this house. I do the flowers in the church every week. And that's how much he thinks of me.

It's pretty clear he's taken sides, and it isn't yours.

EMMA. 'Yours'?

MAM. What?

Long pause.

MAM *suddenly comes to her senses.*

Please don't tell Dad I said anything. I shouldn't have done that. I shouldn't have said anything. He'll kill me if he finds out, or he'll…

Beat.

EMMA. He'll divorce you.

Beat.

MAM. And what'll become of us then?

Beat.

Please, Emma, I just… I don't know how much more I can take.

MAM *looks at* EMMA *imploringly.*

EMMA. I'm not going to say anything.

Mam, I'm –

The phone rings again. They let it ring out.

MAM. We're under siege.

MAM *walks out and goes to bed.*

EMMA *hurriedly takes the wine glass and wine bottle to dispose of.*

She takes the key and takes her tablet. She might consider taking more.

Scene Seven

EMMA. My dreams are heavy, bloated things. It's always the
same now, the world turning sideways, oily black ink
spilling down the walls and flooding the square box that I'm
trapped in, pooling around my ankles, then my knees, then
my chest, until it's over my head and I can't breathe.

I'm told it's important to process the memories, *it's
important to feel your feelings, Emma*. But I don't even
know what I actually remember, what are real memories,
what are mine, and what's been implanted inside there by the
Easy Emma page, and Ms McCarthy, and the guards, and
Bryan, and Ali and Maggie, and my parents, and the
newspapers, and the outraged callers to the radio.

My mother, her voice somewhere between a scream and a
sob, and how she looked at me. That memory is mine. After
all the years of wishing my mother was different, that she
would leave me alone, I am panicked at the idea of her
giving up on me.

I think of school corridors, people parting like the Red Sea,
shoulders banging into mine and then the whispers,
whispers, whispers, *slut*, *liar*, *skank*, *bitch*, *whore*.
Screenshots of those photos printed out and stuffed in my
locker. Ali, Maggie and Zoe not talking to me; it was early
days then, the guards hadn't approached them for their
witness statements yet, they didn't know what I was
alleging. They didn't know about *that word*, so I was still a
disloyal slut. Lunch eaten on my own in a toilet cubicle, new
graffiti on the wall, about me. Is that me?

Dizziness, my knees sliding on the damp floor of the club
toilets – I went there to escape *that word*, falling in a slump
over the cistern, a fist banging on the door, the silence when
I open the door and the person outside sees that it's me. My
face smeared in the bathroom's mirrors. Cold air outside, a
wind cutting through me, arms linked with some faceless
man, ignoring my phone ringing and ringing. On my knees
again, in an alleyway, the concrete cold and hard. I try to

reclaim that night. I try to make new memories to replace the ones that were stolen from me. I try to make it my choice, my decision.

It could be another two years before it comes to trial. Two years. Seven hundred and thirty days. Will every one of them be the same? The crushing disappointment when I awake and find myself still alive. Seven hundred and thirty breakfasts where my father rushed out the door before I can wake up so he doesn't have to look at me. Seven hundred and thirty days with microwaved meals for dinner, watching my father stare suspiciously at the food, biting his lip to not ask my mother what the hell this is, staring out at the overgrown vegetable garden, choked with weeds, then glancing at me, so quick you'd almost miss it. But I always catch him, because I hope he'll look at me and it'll be the way it was before, *you're my princess*. Two years of watching them... watch each other... and then what? Tearing away at each other until there's nothing left.

In two years I'll be twenty-one. I thought I would be in college by then. I imagined myself in winter, wrapped in a duffel coat coming back to my student accommodation with a book under one arm and a takeaway coffee in another. I saw myself in summer in bare legs on the campus lawn, with my new friends, my new romances, my new... life.

I never thought this would be my life; the small, small world of this house with no escape. There is no escape.

Scene Eight

BRYAN *and* MAM *sit for dinner.*

Awkward pause.

BRYAN. Where's Emma?

> *Beat.*

> EMMA!

MAM. Okay, let's go ahead.

> It'll go cold.

> Let's eat while it's hot.

> *They start to eat.*

> EMMA *enters.*

BRYAN. Your eyes are all red.

EMMA. Mine?

BRYAN. Yeah, and your face is puffy.

EMMA. Is it?

BRYAN. You okay?

> *Beat.* MAM *looks at* EMMA.

EMMA. I mustn't have slept very well.

> *Beat.*

> I was restless.

BRYAN. Mam, doesn't Emma looked wrecked?

> *Beat.* MAM *looks at* EMMA *guiltily, looks away.*

MAM. Might be the changing weather.

BRYAN (*to* EMMA). Do you take those vitamins you used to take?

MAM. I don't buy them any more.

BRYAN. It's all a racket anyhow.

Beat.

This is lovely.

EMMA. Yeah.

MAM. It's a bit overdone, but.

BRYAN. No, it's... great.

They push their food around a bit.

It's a pity we're not all here to enjoy it.

MAM. It's usually only Emma, Dad and I on a Monday.

So, usually, we're not all here anyhow.

DAD *enters.*

He starts to take off his jacket.

Pause.

BRYAN. Is this a regular thing now, Dad?

DAD. You're still here, I see, Bryan.

BRYAN. I thought I'd stay around for a while.

DAD (*a bit of bite in his tone*). Right-oh.

BRYAN. You're an hour and a half late.

EMMA *and* MAM *look at him to be quiet.*

DAD. I got held up at work.

BRYAN. You got held up, or you chose to get held up?

DAD. I got held up.

Thank you for dinner, love.

He kisses MAM *on the cheek and she smiles.*

He sits, and they resume eating, silently.

Salt?

MAM *passes it.*

Pause.

BRYAN. I've been trying to learn the guitar again.

Maybe next time I'm home I'll bring it with me and we could try some stuff out.

Em?

EMMA. I don't like singing any more.

BRYAN. You could play piano?

EMMA. I was never any good at piano.

BRYAN. You could practise.

Or take down Mam and Nanny's old violin?

EMMA. Maybe.

DAD. Like Nero.

BRYAN. What?

Beat.

MAM. Emma lost her confidence with all that when she was thirteen.

That's what happens to girls.

BRYAN. That's not a fact, is it?

Or… some other kind of hobby. You always said that, Dad.

MAM. Emma, you're barely eating.

EMMA. I can't taste anything.

DAD. Is your face swollen?

DAD looks at MAM. MAM looks away guiltily. No one says anything. Resumes eating.

Beat.

BRYAN. Do we eat in silence now?

MAM. We're tired, love.

DAD. Actually. Okay.

Beat.

I have some news.

Beat. EMMA *sits up.*

BRYAN. What news?

DAD. Well.

BRYAN. Did they plead guilty?

EMMA. Did they?

BRYAN. Did someone do the honest thing?

Beat.

DAD. No, it's not. Uh. The area manager came into the branch today.

We had to discuss the spate of recent transfers from the bank.

Beat.

There's been a lot of account transfers from the bank, and they've made a decision.

MAM. That's not your fault.

DAD. Someone's got to take the fall, and they made their decision.

BRYAN. What decision?

DAD. They're transferring me to another bank, in the city. The assistant manager in Douglas is retiring, so they / think –

BRYAN. Assistant?

DAD. It's… a bigger branch than Ballinatoom.

It's fine.

MAM. But, you built that place.

DAD. Plenty of young guys coming up well capable of doing just as good a job.

I have a job, still, and we should be grateful for that, in this climate, and in the… circumstances.

Pause.

So that's that. I just wanted you all to know. Now you know.

Beat. He resumes eating.

(*Slightly cutting, looking away.*) Now, what were you saying about singing, Bryan?

They all resume eating. BRYAN *feels the sting of the last remark.*

Long silence.

EMMA (*to audience*). I have done this.

(*Doesn't realise she's spoken out loud.*) What's the point then?

MAM. Point of what?

Beat.

Emma?

EMMA (*to audience*). I didn't want to ruin anyone's life.

BRYAN. Are you okay?

EMMA. No. Yeah. No. I'm not.

I have news, too.

I've made a decision… I've decided to withdraw my complaint.

Beat.

She gets up and scrapes her dinner into the bin.

BRYAN. Emma, sit down.

She pauses, she turns around.

EMMA. Did you hear me? I'm going to withdraw my complaint.

MAM. We heard you.

Beat. MAM *and* DAD *look at each other.*

EMMA. Well, what do you think?

Beat. BRYAN *looks at parents.*

DAD. I don't know, Emma.

Beat. He considers his words.

This is something you'd have to consider very seriously.

EMMA. I am serious.

I'm... never going to win... am I?

EMMA waits hesitatingly, imploringly, for them to respond.

MAM. Well... it might.

Beat. She looks at DAD.

It might be easier.

Better. Better, I mean, for you. If that's what you want.

EMMA. Yeah, I...

Her parents look at each other and resume eating.

EMMA looks lost.

BRYAN. What, is this fucking it?

(*To* EMMA.) After all this, you're just going to give up?

EMMA. Maybe.

BRYAN. Emma.

MAM. She's not giving up, she's –

BRYAN. Is this what you *actually* want?

EMMA flounders.

It's not, is it?

Even if you do withdraw your complaint, what's to say the DPP won't prosecute anyway? They're doing it on behalf of the state, right?

EMMA (*to* DAD). They can't make me do it if I don't want to, can they?

DAD. I don't know. I can call Aidan Heffernan tomorrow.

BRYAN. They might still be able to use your statement. And the photos...

MAM. We don't even know if they would admit those photos in court, I told you that. There's no precedent.

BRYAN. So we should make a precedent, no? What if this happens to someone else?

MAM. I'm sure it won't. They're good boys really. This all just got out of hand.

Beat. EMMA *starts.*

BRYAN. What the fuck did you just say?

MAM. I didn't mean it like that. Emma, you know I didn't mean it like –

DAD. Lower your voice, Bryan.

BRYAN. Okay, forgetting the disgusting piece of shit she just came out with, that the animals who fucking gang-raped my sister and posted photos on Facebook for the whole world to laugh at, are actually – I can't even say it – tell me this, what about Emma? What's going to happen to her now?

DAD. Hah?

BRYAN. She's not getting better. When was the last time she went to school?

MAM. She's being homeschooled.

BRYAN *laughs harshly.*

BRYAN. Oh really? So she's going to be sitting her Leaving, is she? And where's she going to do that? Is she going to do it in St Brigid's? Has she got her exam number? How did her mocks go? Has she filled out her CAO form? What college is she hoping to go to? What course is she thinking of doing? Where's she going to live? Come on, Mam, if you're homeschooling her, you should be able to tell me all of this, shouldn't you?

MAM.

BRYAN. You don't know, because *you've* given up on her. Both of you.

Pause. EMMA *waits again for her parents to speak. They don't.*

When was the last time she went outside? At least when it first happened, she still went to school, she met up with her friends, she had a fucking life –

MAM. The therapist says that's normal. Lots of people who claim to be raped can be strangely calm at the beginning.

EMMA *lurches again.*

BRYAN. Claim? Did you honestly just say 'claim'?

MAM. You know what I mean, Bryan!

BRYAN. Oh my / God.

MAM. We're not all as up to date on the language of all of this / you know –

BRYAN. Did you see photographic evidence of Dylan Walsh pissing on her / and say 'claim'?

MAM. We don't always have the, the right thing to say –

BRYAN. I can't believe I'm hearing this. In our own house.

They can't get away with this; I can't believe you would even think about letting Emma do this.

EMMA. Bryan, it's honestly maybe best.

BRYAN. It's not best.

I have to go back and listen to lads laugh about this? In the pub, have a crack at it. It'll be a joke again. Just a joke. A girl called rape cos she was embarrassed and then got chicken about seeing it through. Nothing will fucking change. When it's your fucking sister. Your daughter?

DAD. This isn't about you.

BRYAN. Emma, please, please don't do this.

(*To parents.*) What is wrong with you both?

Is this about sex? Do you think it was wrong she had sex at all?

DAD. This isn't appropriate.

BRYAN. I don't give a *shit* what's appropriate.

They *used* her like a doll, they humiliated her and they *enjoyed* it. They thought it was funny. They actually thought this was funny.

And they think they're going to get away with it, they're cool as anything about this right now.

Hah? Nothing?

Look at her. Someone has to pay for this.

Pause.

Emma? Emma, come on.

Beat.

EMMA. Maybe I did want it.

Beat.

BRYAN. You didn't.

EMMA. How do you know?

BRYAN. I know.

EMMA. I went into that room.

BRYAN. Not for that.

EMMA. But for something. I wanted something.

BRYAN. Not for *that*.

EMMA. How do I *know* what?

Maybe I just went along with it and said rape afterwards to make you not hate me. Maybe it *was* all a joke. Maybe I allowed it to happen to me.

BRYAN. No, Emma.

EMMA. I don't know, I don't remember.

BRYAN. You can't give... consent... if you're unconscious –
that's just a fact –

EMMA. Veronica Horan wrote something, something about
women –

BRYAN. Veronica Horan is a psychopath, whom you shouldn't
be reading –

EMMA. Women imagining they were abused, like Freud said it
or something, and it was actually fantasy, and they thought it
was real, but it was –

BRYAN. No, rubbish, that's bogus. He wrote that shitty theory
because otherwise everyone would have to reckon with how
many women and children were actually being abused –

DAD. That's enough now, enough of the hysterics.

EMMA (*to* BRYAN). What are they going to say in trial?

They're going to say that I changed my statement. I said it
was a joke initially and then I –

BRYAN. Yeah, because you were afraid.

You were in shock.

You wanted it to go away, that's a natural –

EMMA. Bryan, please! You can go and have a normal life now.
You can finish college and meet someone new, a nice girl, far
away from this town, and you can get married to her and tell
her all about this some night, in a restaurant, and cry and she'll
hold you and she'll say it's okay, and you can, over time, forget
about this, and bring your kids home here to Mam and Dad,
and they can love them, and you can have a normal life.

BRYAN. I can do that anyway.

I can do all that anyway, Em, what are you talking –

DAD. Stop, Bryan! You want to sacrifice your sister for a
principle in a fight she is very unlikely to win?

Real life isn't ideal, you'll see that yourself soon enough.

BRYAN. No, this is about you two, not her.

Emma needs us to –

DAD. *Emma* will tell us what she needs.

You have to respect Emma's decision.

BRYAN (*pleadingly, with emotion*). But Dad, please, listen to me we have a responsibility –

DAD. I said stop it now! Talk about responsibility now! Who was Emma left with this time last year? Where was your responsibility then? Too busy with your own woman to care about your sister.

BRYAN (*upset*). Dad.

MAM. Denis, stop.

DAD. Have some respect in your own house to your own father. (*He could almost square up to* BRYAN.)

If I *ever* spoke to my parents like that. And thank god they're not here to see any of this. Thank god!

MAM. Denis, okay –

DAD. The shame of it would kill them.

BRYAN *throws his arms up at this last comment too, and backs away from* DAD.

DAD *turns and looks at* EMMA *directly, the first time in months to do so.*

Emma, Emmie.

Look at me.

Is this what you want?

Long pause. She looks between them all. This is not what she wants.

EMMA (*to audience*). What I want.

No.

I want you to take my hand, and to look at me. To say you haven't given up on me, that you love me, and that you will fight for me. Fight for me every day for the rest of your lives, for ever if that's what it takes, because I am worth fighting for, I am worth something. I am your daughter, your girl, and this is not my fault.

I want you to say you believe me. Do you believe me? Did you ever believe me?

But they look at me, *say yes, say yes, say yes*.

DAD *goes to her in a tender gesture we have never seen him do before*.

DAD. Look at me, princess.

Beat.

Is this what you want?

She looks at BRYAN *emotionally and then back at her father*.

EMMA. Yes.

Yes, this is what I want.

BRYAN *weeps as* DAD *hugs her. We might see* BRYAN *get his bag and leave in the transition*.

Scene Nine

EMMA *in her bedroom, mirroring the first scene*.

MAM (*from outside*). Emma, can I come in?

She comes in.

I made scones.

I made them from the old Darina recipe.

EMMA. Okay.

MAM. Do you want to come down, Dad would like us to have breakfast together.

Of course he wants to wait for the DPP to get back to him, before we really celebrate.

EMMA. Okay.

Beat.

MAM. Dad and I are very proud of you.

EMMA. Yeah.

MAM. We can put this behind us now.

EMMA. Yeah.

MAM. We can… forget this happened and move on. Everyone has… setbacks.

Everyone has… stuff in their past. They. They put it behind them, and they move on. You know? Lots of people… You have to keep moving, don't you?

Beat.

Well, whenever you're ready, we'll be downstairs.

She's about to go.

EMMA. Where's Bryan?

Beat.

MAM. He's gone back to Limerick. We're paying enough for him to be up there at college. He needs to… get on with it.

Beat.

EMMA. He never said goodbye.

MAM. …He had to leave early. He'll call you soon, he said.

EMMA. Okay. I'll follow down.

MAM. Okay, love.

She looks at her.

You look beautiful this morning, Emmie.

Pause. She looks away. As if to convince herself.

I have a beautiful family.

She leaves.

EMMA. Bryan has left my laptop on a chair, the lead wrapping around it to keep it shut. I unwind it. I see albums emerging now of Graduation Ceremony, everyone crying and hugging with the teachers, signing each other's school shirts, taking funny pictures in the lab and on the tennis court. Then they're back at Dylan Walsh's epic party; Sean, Ali, Eli, Maggie and… Zoe are there. Maggie and Eli are holding hands. They must be back together.

Conor emails. He's sorry to hear my decision. He wishes he could have protected me. He wishes he could go back to that night too, he wishes he had kissed me, like he wanted to.

Maybe I should have kissed him that night, at the party. I could have kissed him, and we could have stayed in while the others went to the party. We might have watched a movie with Bryan and Jen, groaning when they went to bed and Bryan telling us not to do anything he wouldn't do. I'd have taken my clothes off before him, and watched his face as he looked at me like I was the most beautiful girl in the world. I could have let him love me. We could have fallen in love. I might have been happy.

EMMA *strips to her underwear and investigates herself in the mirror.*

I belong to those boys now, as surely as if they have stamped me with a cattle brand. They have seared their names into my heart.

The pre-recorded voices may be EMMA*'s, or boys', as she looks in the mirror.*

VOICE. Fuck, Emma O'Donovan's tits are tiny though. I thought they'd be way better than that.

VOICE 2. Her ass looks good though.

VOICE. I would.

VOICE 2. Not any more. Would you?

VOICE. Too many fingers in that pie.

VOICE (*meaning 'fuck', said in an almost admiring tone*).
I'd fucking destroy her.

Laughs.

EMMA *makes eye contact with the girl in the mirror.*

MAM (*offstage*). Emmie?

Emma, Dad's leaving soon!

Pause.

EMMA. I'm coming.

Pause.

Okay, I'm coming now.

She doesn't move.

The house begins to move, it packs up around her, her parents resume their rituals.

We see footage of her friends at graduation, moving on. ZOE close up, or ZOE in a light like at the top of the play, getting results to go to college. Or a shot of college campus and leaves and freedom, etc. Boys back on the sports field (or throwing a ball on the outskirts of the stage). The world moves in fast-forward motion.

EMMA *stays still. She is left behind.*

EMMA *stares at us. She mouths something we can't hear.*

Lights down.

End of Play.

A Nick Hern Book

This stage adaptation of *Asking for It* first published in Great Britain in 2018 as a paperback original by Nick Hern Books Limited, The Glasshouse, 49a Goldhawk Road, London W12 8QP, in association with Landmark Productions and The Everyman

Asking for It copyright © 2015 Louise O'Neill
First published by Quercus Publishing Ltd in 2015

This stage adaptation of *Asking for It* copyright © 2018 Meadhbh McHugh with Annabelle Comyn

Meadhbh McHugh with Annabelle Comyn have asserted their right to be identified as the authors of this adaptation

Cover photography by Hugh O'Conor

Designed and typeset by Nick Hern Books, London
Printed in Great Britain by Mimeo Ltd, Huntingdon, Cambridgeshire PE29 6XX

A CIP catalogue record for this book is available from the British Library

ISBN 978 1 84842 820 1

www.nickhernbooks.co.uk

facebook.com/nickhernbooks

twitter.com/nickhernbooks